Reader's Digest

FAMILY SONGBOOK

Pleasure-programmed for your greater entertainment

W. A. H. Birnie, Editor
Letitia B. Kehoe, Associate Editor
William L. Simon, Project Editor

Music arranged and edited by Dan Fox
Introductions to songs by Stanley Green

The Reader's Digest Association, Inc.
Pleasantville, New York   Montreal

Copyright © 1969 The Reader's Digest Association, Inc.
Copyright © 1969 The Reader's Digest Association (Canada) Ltd.

Unauthorized reproduction, in any manner, is prohibited.

Library of Congress Catalog Card Number 70-84403
ISBN 0-89577-002-4

READER'S DIGEST and the Pegasus logo are registered trademarks
of The Reader's Digest Association, Inc.

Printed in the United States of America

Twelfth Printing, August 1991

Guide to More Fun
from Your Song Book

Listening is one thing, but performing means really participating in music, becoming an integral part of it, almost like the composer. Everybody enjoys hearing music over the radio or on records; we even make folk heroes out of unusually gifted interpreters of songs, whether singers or instrumentalists. Yet there is nothing about music so satisfying as the involvement of playing and singing great songs together. Great in the sense of nostalgic and soaring melodies, rhythmic dances, inspirational hymns—all the glittering facets of the musical diamond.

This wonderful involvement in music is what the *Reader's Digest Family Song Book* is all about. Here, we give you a unique collection of 124 favorites for endless evenings of fun, relaxation and excitement. And this is what we mean when we say *unique*: In no other song book will you find a selection of songs so provocatively programmed, with such easy and adaptable arrangements, with surprising musical twists which you will find simple to play but will delight your friends. We're really proud not only of the songs we have selected but of the way we're presenting them to you. And we're sure you will be pleased, too, when you run through the first few of these up-to-the-minute arrangements.

Actually, simply by opening it, you'll see one reason why the Song Book is something special. Rather than being stitched and bound together, the pages are hinged on a spiral binding that allows them to lie flat on a music rack. The result: no need to flatten down pages yourself and no danger of damaging the book's spine. Also, of the 124 selections included, no less than 113 have been so organized that they fit completely on either one or two pages, thereby eliminating page turning in the middle of a song. This has been accomplished not by reducing the size of the typeface but by omitting the rarely played introductory verses or forestrains as well as any superfluous harmonic embellishments that might prove difficult for the average performer. The more experienced performer will probably want to add his own elaborations anyhow.

Selecting just the right songs for a well-balanced compendium resulted in a list of 124 songs that constitute virtually an all-time musical Hit Parade. These are the songs that are almost as meaningful to us as pictures in a family album or pages in a diary. We have danced to them, sung them in schools, on birthdays, at picnic sing-alongs, at family reunions, and at all kinds of social events. There's hardly one here that will fail to stir your memory of some long-ago happening.

We hope we've also increased your enjoyment of this Song Book with the introductory paragraphs you'll find with the songs in the book. These are crammed with little-known stories about how a song was born, how it was introduced to the public, what musical and lyrical qualities have given the song its distinction. Some players may want to read them aloud before the group singing gets underway.

To make sure that these songs appear in the most useful and enjoyable way possible, the editors have been guided by the concept of Pleasure Programming. One of the features of this unique and exclusive Reader's Digest approach to music is to group together songs with common chronological and musical traits. In this book, they fall into eight major categories:

1. *Down Memory Lane* . . . Those wonderfully nostalgic numbers we associate with the Roaring Twenties, or the periods just before and after. These were the favorites of World War I, the carefree days of the Jazz Age, and the chins-up sentiments of the Depression years.

2. *All-Time Broadway Hit Parade* . . . Memorable music and lyrics from the pens of the acknowledged giants of musical comedy: George and Ira Gershwin, Richard Rodgers and Lorenz Hart, Howard Dietz and Arthur Schwartz, Cole Porter, Vincent Youmans, Kurt Weill and others—a musical tour behind the footlights of the Golden Age of the American Musical Theater.

3. *Great Music from the Movies* . . . Unforgettable themes from dramatic hits, and hit tunes from the screen's happiest musicals . . . Fond recollections of Dick Powell swooning over Ruby Keeler, Humphrey Bogart mooning over Ingrid Bergman, Doris Day all sugar and cream, and the magnolia-drenched grandeur of Scarlett O'Hara's beloved plantation, Tara.

4. *The Swing Years* . . . Back to the late Thirties and early Forties when swing was king . . . Latter-day Pied Pipers such as Tommy Dorsey, Louis Armstrong, Guy Lombardo, the Andrews Sisters and Bob Crosby luring us with their danceable numbers, ideal for either cheek-to-cheeking or jitter-bugging.

5. *A Treasury of Operetta and Semi-Classical Hits* . . . The world of Victor Herbert, Sigmund Romberg and Franz Lehár, full of rich melodies and robust rhythms . . . Songs that are sung in those floridly romantic musicals that never lose their appeal no matter how often they are revived.

6. *Gaslight Varieties* . . . Turning the clock back to the turn of the century, and even before . . . The charm and innocence of a bygone day captured in the lilting pieces our great-grandparents used to sing.

7. *Greensleeves and Other Folk Song Favorites* . . . Encompassing the widest chronological range of all—from Elizabethan ballads and country dance tunes right up to their modern counterparts written and sung by the leading balladeers of our day.

8. *Music to Lift the Spirit* . . . The hymns and anthems that sustain us in good times and bad . . . Patriotic airs celebrating our country's greatness, not just on the battlefield but also in the majestic, peaceful heartland.

Pleasure Programming, however, doesn't stop with placing songs in these congenial categories. We provide you here with lots more cross-references to help you round out particular moods and occasions. Here you will find the most suitable numbers for dancing, each with the tempo and dance type indicated. Here too are songs for marching, nostalgic songs and glad songs, songs for the particular girl and songs for the particular boy, songs to open amateur musicals and songs to close them, and songs for different types of group singing (all the way from a barbershop quartet to a community sing-along). More special requirements? The Song Book provides you with listings of songs associated with weddings, Ireland, months, days and seasons.

And for those who like their music unobtrusively in the background there are two medley collections: one "light and lively," the other "soft, sweet and soothing." To gain maximum benefit from this aspect of Pleasure Programming, why not attach cards, clips or other markings on the desired pages ahead of time and make the programs run more smoothly?

All the arrangements have been especially created to provide easy-to-play fingering so that the average parlor musician can perform to his best advantage. Many of the pieces, chiefly the older standards, have been updated for the first time through the use of smooth, modern harmonies and intriguing rhythmic effects.

Note, too, that each song has been arranged for three instruments: piano, guitar and organ. However, these arrangements can easily be adapted to any treble-clef C instrument, such as accordion, chromatic harmonica, violin, flute, mandolin, banjo, ukulele, recorder, marimba and xylophone. Most of them can also be used for the chord organ.

Any guitarist—or would-be guitarist—need only read the special guitar diagrams above the staves to be able to accompany the songs. As for the organist, he should have no trouble finding the proper organ pedal merely by reading the small notes on the bass clef.

Also in the area of simplification, the songs may be performed on a keyboard instrument by playing the melody with the right hand and following the chord symbols to improvise a left-hand accompaniment. Piano students will probably recognize this as the "popular piano" method widely used by music teachers today.

It is also important to note that, in order to distinguish the melody from other symbols for the right hand, the stem of each melody note goes *upward* unless it stands alone.

A song book, of course, can simplify the arrangements, but it cannot play them. It can be a teaching aid, but it cannot teach. Nonetheless, everything possible has been done to assure the amateur musician's fullest enjoyment and proficiency. The rest is up to you . . . Experienced pianists who have played these arrangements tell us, "The notes seem to fall right under your fingers—no need for reaching or stretching."

We hope you feel the same way about it.

The Editors

Index to Songs

* * * Index to Composers * * *

Index to Lyricists

Pleasure Programs
(pages 7-9)

I SING-ALONG FUN

II LET'S DANCE!
(Tempos and Types)

MEDIUM FOX TROTS

Avalon

In 1921, opera composer Giacomo Puccini brought suit against the publisher of "Avalon," charging that the melody had been lifted from his aria "E lucevan le stelle" in Tosca. *He walked out of the courthouse $25,000 richer. Apparently the resulting publicity only made "Avalon" more popular, and today it still exerts its siren-call appeal. The song was closely identified with Al Jolson.*

Words by Al Jolson and B. G. DeSylva

Music by Vincent Rose

Tip-Toe Thru the Tulips with Me

One of the earliest color-splashed screen musicals was Gold Diggers of Broadway, *a 1929 extravaganza that produced the song hit of the year, "Tip-Toe Thru the Tulips with Me."*

Words by Al Dubin   Music by Joe Burke

Moderately, with a lilt

mf

Tip-toe to the win-dow, by the win-dow, That is where I'll be, Come

Tip-Toe Thru The Tu-lips With Me.

Tip-toe from your pil-low, to the shad-ow of a wil-low tree, And

13

Memory Lane

Lyric writer Buddy DeSylva was uncannily tuned to the public's moods and longings. The songwriting trio he formed with Ray Henderson and Lew Brown virtually dominated Tin Pan Alley between 1926 and 1931, but still each member found time to turn out hits with other writers as well. In 1924 DeSylva teamed with Spier and Conrad for one song — one dreamy, nostalgic, enduring masterpiece.

Words by B. G. DeSylva

Music by Larry Spier and Con Conrad

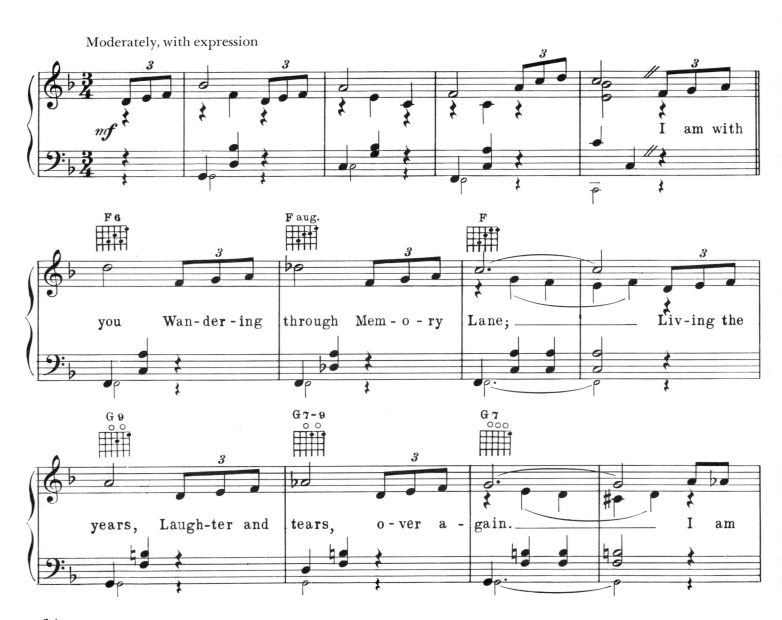

dream - ing yet of the night we met When life was a love - ly re - frain. You were so shy Say-ing "Good-by" there in the dawn; On - ly a glance Full of ro - mance, and you were gone! Though my dreams are in vain, My love will re - main Stroll-ing a - gain, Mem-o-ry Lane, with you. *slower*

15

Bye Bye Blackbird

Every new generation seems susceptible to this carefree, rhythmic charmer of a song. Perhaps it's because the lyrics, though virtually a string of non sequiturs, convey the feeling of thumbing one's nose at the whole darned complicated, oppressive world. In the year 1926, composer Henderson could afford to do this. "Blackbird" was one of five hits he had written in that year, equaling his track record of the previous year.

Words by Mort Dixon   **Music by Ray Henderson**

Ain't She Sweet

Words by
Jack Yellen

In 1959, Jack Yellen attended the 50th anniversary of his high-school graduating class. As writer of "Ain't She Sweet" (1926) and dozens of other hit songs, he was somewhat of a celebrity. But his one-time English teacher was unimpressed. "So you're the one who wrote 'Ain't She Sweet,'" she said. "And I thought I taught you that 'ain't' is bad grammar!"

Music by
Milton Ager

Moderately, with a bounce

Ain't She Sweet? See her com-ing down the street! Now I ask you ver-y con-fi-den-tial-ly Ain't She Sweet?

Ain't she nice? Look her o-ver once or twice. Now I

IF YOU WERE
THE ONLY GIRL IN THE WORLD

England's famed comic George Robey first posed this melodic hypothesis in the 1916 London musical The Bing Boys Are Here. *It floundered along for about 13 years until Rudy Vallee got a bright idea: He changed its beat from a fox trot to a waltz and successfully reintroduced it in his movie debut,* The Vagabond Lover.

Words by Clifford Grey   **Music by Nat D. Ayer**

Carolina in the Morning

The 1920s saw a great profusion of songs celebrating the appeal of the Southland. Though Kahn and Donaldson had never been in either Carolina when they penned this tribute, their adroit combination of hopping and skipping notes, internal rhymes and tongue-twisting descriptions produced an irresistible travel brochure.

Words by Gus Kahn

Music by Walter Donaldson

Noth - ing could be fin - er than to be in Car - o - li - na In The Morn - ing, No one could be sweet-er than my

But-ter-flies all flut-ter up and kiss each lit-tle but-ter-cup at

dawn - ing, If I had A-lad-din's lamp for

on-ly a day,___ I'd make a wish and here's what I'd say:___

Noth-ing could be fin-er than to be in Car-o-li-na In The

Morn - ing.___

Moonlight Bay

Words by Edward Madden

Music by Percy Wenrich

In 1912, just one year after "Alexander's Ragtime Band" had stirred up the country, Messrs. Madden and Wenrich helped lull it back to the calm waters of "Moonlight Bay." Two other imperishables from Wenrich: "Put on Your Old Grey Bonnet" and "When You Wore a Tulip."

We were sail-ing a - long On Moon-light Bay, We could hear the voic-es ring - ing, They seemed to say: "You have sto-len my heart, Now don't go 'way!" As we sang Love's Old Sweet Song On Moon-light Bay.

I Wonder What's Become of Sally

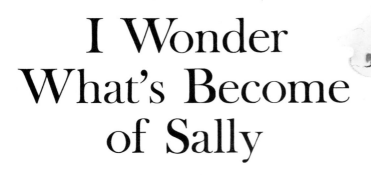

Many popular songs have begat other popular songs. After "Sally, Won't You Come Home" had scored a hit in the Ziegfeld Follies of 1921, Yellen and Ager were inspired to write their own ballad about the much-missed lady, "I Wonder What's Become of Sally." They even got the same singer, Joe Schenck of Van and Schenck, to introduce their song. The new "Sally" not only eclipsed the first, it sold over a million copies of sheet music.

Words by Jack Yellen   **Music by Milton Ager**

Ev - er since the day Sal - ly went a - way. No

mat - ter what she is, Wher - ev - er she may be, If

mf a tempo and rather more rhythmically

no one wants her now Please send her home to me. I'll

rall.

al - ways wel - come back my Sal - ly, That

mp rather freely, as before

old gal of mine!

rall.

Melody

Pretty Baby

Though four annual editions had preceded it on Broadway, The Passing Show of 1916 *became the first revue of the series to produce a genuine song hit: "Pretty Baby." Actually, this Kahn-Jackson-Van Alstyne number was an interpolation, since the nominal composer for the revue—as he was for seven of the 14 annual* Passing Shows*—was Sigmund Romberg. But Romberg never managed to produce even one hit song for the series.*

**Words by
Gus Kahn**

Music by Tony Jackson and Egbert Van Alstyne

Ev - 'ry - bod - y loves a ba - by that's why I'm in love with you, Pret - ty Ba - by, Pret - ty Ba - by. And I'd

April Showers

When the great Al Jolson was in a Broadway show, audiences didn't care a bit about the story of the musical. The all-important attraction was their beloved Jolie singing and clowning to his—and their—hearts' content. So it was with Bombo, a 1921 hit that opened at a spanking new theater named in Jolson's honor. The nightly showstopper, which Jolson sang from a platform jutting right into the audience, was "April Showers."

Words by B. G. DeSylva   **Music by Louis Silvers**

Though A - pril Show - ers _ may come your way, _ They bring the flow - ers that bloom in May. _ So if it's rain - ing have no re - grets, _

I'm Forever Blowing Bubbles

If the name Kenbrovin seems a bit unusual it's only because it was the pseudonym of no less than three writers— James Kendis, James Brockman and Nat Vincent. Contracting their first names may have presented a problem, but their last names lent themselves equitably and smoothly to the abbreviations of "Ken," "bro" and "vin." In their song celebrating the pleasures of idling away one's time on daydreams and fantasies, the writers deliberately created a theme similar to a hit of the previous year, "I'm Always Chasing Rainbows."

Words and Music by Jaan Kenbrovin and John William Kellette

Smiles

Words by J. Will Callahan

Music by Lee S. Roberts

Composer Roberts got the happy notion to write a song about smiles after hearing a lecture on the subject at a music-dealers' convention. Unveiled in 1917, it became a perfect morale booster for both soldiers and civilians, possibly all the more welcome because it avoided pointless optimism. "Smiles" was interpolated in The Passing Show of 1918.

smiles that steal a-way the tear - drops ____ As the sun - beams steal a-way the dew; ____ There are smiles that have a ten-der mean - ing ____ That the eyes of love a-lone may see, ____ And the smiles that fill my life with sun - shine ____ Are the smiles that you give to me.

There's a Long, Long Trail

Words by Stoddard King

Music by Zo Elliott

Evenly, with much expression

There's A Long, Long Trail a - wind - ing In - to the land of my dreams, Where the night - in - gales are

Despite its close identification with World War I, this song was actually composed the year before war was declared. Elliott and King were then Yale undergraduates and created it as nothing more than a sentimental piece to be sung at a fraternity banquet. First published in England, it was sung and marched to by British Tommies well before being picked up by American doughboys when they went to fight in Europe in 1917.

My Buddy

While there has always seemed to be something redolent of World War I about "My Buddy," the tender waltz was actually not written until 1922, the year in which lyricist Kahn first began his fruitful collaboration with composer Donaldson. Created in the traditional 32-bar form, the song was made up of two 16-bar sections identical in melody except for the closing bars.

Words by Gus Kahn **Music by Walter Donaldson**

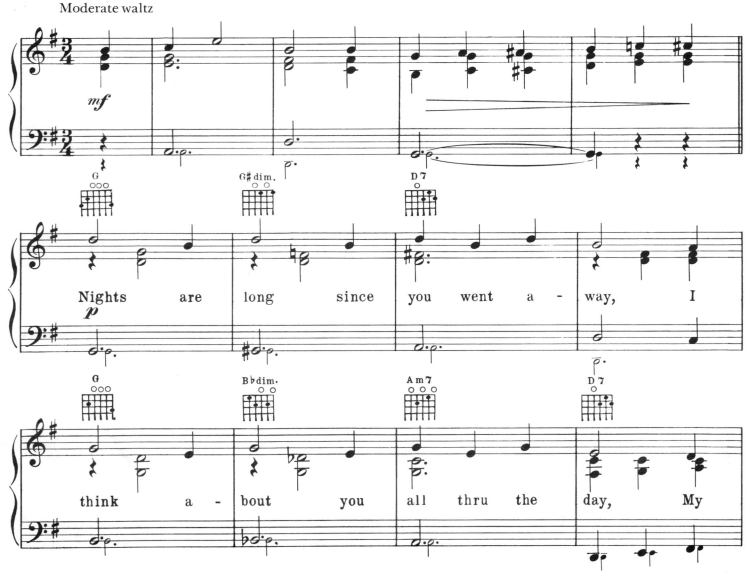

I'm Looking Over a Four Leaf Clover

First offered in 1927, this song was pretty well overlooked until 1948, the year bandleader Art Mooney recorded it in a razzmatazzy arrangement. When, through a whim, disc jockey Al "Jazzbo" Collins decided to play it continuously one afternoon over a Salt Lake City radio station, the event generated enough front-page publicity throughout the country to boost both the record and sheet-music sales to best-seller status.

**Words by
Mort Dixon**

**Music by
Harry Woods**

Third is the ros-es that grow in the lane,

No need ex-plain-ing, the one re-main - ing Is

some - bod-y I a - dore.

mp cresc. I'm Look-ing O - ver A Four Leaf Clo - ver that I o-ver-

looked be - fore. (No Chords)

Charleston

The dance sensation that best typified the flamingly youthful spirit of the 1920s was the high-kicking Charleston, which also happened to be the name of a song. Introduced in the 1923 all-Negro revue Runnin' Wild, the dance very soon replaced the shimmy as the favorite gyrational exercise in ballrooms across the nation.

Words and Music by
Cecil Mack
and Jimmy Johnson

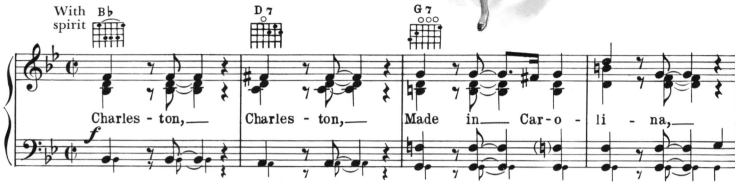

Charles-ton,___ Charles-ton,___ Made in___ Car-o-li - na,___

Some dance,___ Some prance,___ I'll say,___ There's noth-ing fin - er than the

Charles-ton,___ Charles-ton,___ Lord, how___ you can shuf - fle,___

Ev-'ry step___ you do, Leads to some - thing new, Man I'm tell - ing you,

It's a la - pa - zoo, Buck dance,___ Wing dance,___

Will be___ a back num - ber,___ But the Charles-ton,___ The new Charles-ton,___

That dance___ is sure-ly a com - er. Some - time,___ You'll___ dance it

one time,___ The dance___ called the Charles-ton,___ Made in South___ Car-o-

line!

In a Shanty in Old Shanty Town

In 1932, when this paean to poverty was written, there were many shanties in many shanty towns throughout the nation. For the country was then in the depth of the Depression and receptive to a lyric celebrating the pleasure of a far from luxurious abode. Co-composer Little Jack Little, who was primarily a pianist and bandleader, introduced the number on his radio program in his intimate half-singing, half-talking style.

Words by Joe Young   **Music by Little Jack Little and John Siras**

tum - bled down shack By an old rail - road track, Like a

mil - lion-aire's man - sion is call - ing me back. I'd give up a

pal - ace if I were a king; It's more than a pal - ace it's

my ev - 'ry - thing. There's a queen wait-ing there with a sil - ver - y

crown, In A Shan-ty In Old Shan-ty Town.

45

"For You" was a mere Hit Parade bystander until it was added to the repertoire of Glen Gray and the Casa Loma Orchestra. Kenny Sargent's almost ethereal delivery made it one of the band's most in-demand selections, and subsequent recordings, such as Rose-

mary Clooney's and Nat "King" Cole's, helped to keep its popularity aloft. In addition to "For You," Dubin and Burke were responsible for such perennial favorites as "Tip-Toe Thru the Tulips With Me" and "Dancing with Tears in My Eyes."

FOR YOU

Words by Al Dubin

Music by Joe Burke

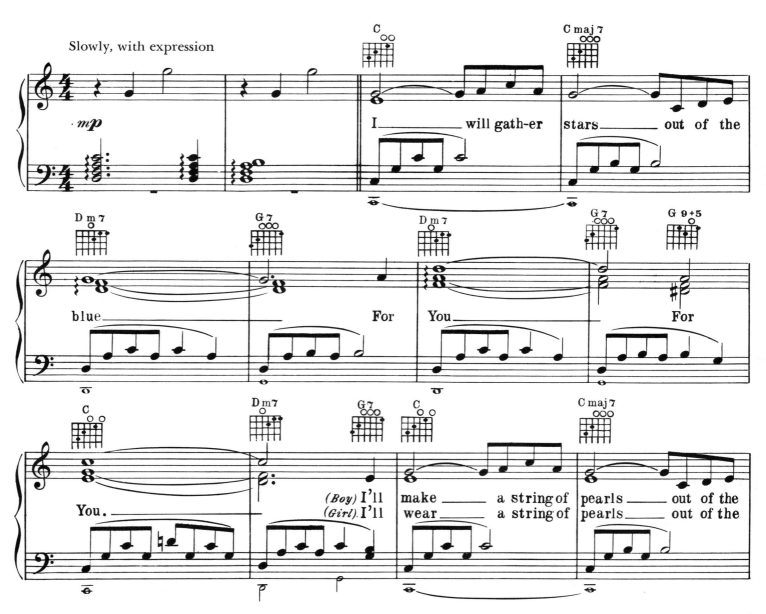

Poor Butterfly

In writing the score for the 1916 Hippodrome spectacle,
The Big Show, *lyricist Golden thought the star would
be Tamaki Miura, who had sung in* Madame Butterfly.
*So he wrote a ballad for her about the opera—only to
discover another soprano had been signed for the show.
Nothing daunted, he mated his lyrics to a melody by
composer Hubbell and, in his words, "Two months later
the entire country was Butterfly-mad."*

Words by John Golden

Music by Raymond Hubbell

If I Could Be with You One Hour Tonight

**Words and Music by
Henry Creamer and Jimmy Johnson**

Apart from the song's unusual brevity (only 16 bars) and odd construction, "If I Could Be with You One Hour Tonight" offers a rare example of a song whose complete title is sung only once—and then not at the anticipated beginning of the refrain. Composer Johnson—also known as James P. Johnson —was a brilliant jazz pianist as well as writer of such standards as "Charleston," "Old-Fashioned Love" and "Runnin' Wild."

-til I told you, Hon-ey, why I love you so.___ If I Could

Be With You One Hour To-night,___ If I was free to do the

things I might,___ I'm tell-ing you true___ I'd be

an-y-thing but blue, If I Could Be With You.___

51

Till We Meet Again

Though "Till We Meet Again" was to become the most popular ballad of World War I, composer Whiting and lyricist Egan thought so little of its commercial chances that they threw the manuscript in a wastebasket. Mrs. Whiting, however, had other ideas. She fished it out and, unknown to her husband, took it to publisher Jerome Remick. Her faith in the song was soon confirmed. Even before the sheet music was off the presses, Remick got the first inkling of the song's future success when it won a war-song contest sponsored by a Detroit movie theater.

Words by Raymond B. Egan   **Music by Richard A. Whiting**

Smile the while you kiss me sad a-dieu,

When the clouds roll by I'll come to you;

When Day Is Done

English version by B. G. DeSylva

Music and original text by Dr. Robert Katcher

Although composer Katcher had written operettas in his native Vienna and later spent more than ten years in Hollywood, his only durable work was "When Day Is Done." Titled "Madonna" when published in Vienna in 1924, it received its English title and lyrics years later.

Softly and gently

When Day Is Done and shad-ows fall, I dream of you; When Day Is Done I think of all the joys we knew. That yearn-ing, re-turn-ing, to hold you in my arms, Won't go love, I know love, With-out you night has lost its charms. When

55

In 1929, as part of their score for an early "talkie" called Chasing Rainbows, Yellen and Ager wrote "Happy Days Are Here Again" to be sung by a group of American doughboys upon receiving news of the armistice. On the night of the Wall Street crash, before the film was released, the writers took the music to George Olsen, then leading his dance orchestra at the Hotel Pennsylvania in New York. As the vocalist sang, the

Happy Days Are Here Again

dispirited diners, according to Yellen, stopped what they were doing and "joined in sardonically, hysterically, like doomed prisoners on their way to the firing squad." The song was quickly picked up as a genuine rallying cry of the Depression years and, in 1932, became the official theme of Franklin D. Roosevelt's victorious campaign for the Presidency.

Words by Jack Yellen

Music by Milton Ager

be no more from now on. Hap - py Days Are Here A - gain! The skies a - bove are clear a - gain, Let us sing a song of cheer a - gain, Hap - py Days Are Here A - gain!

The Man I Love

"The Man I Love" had the odd distinction of becoming a recognized standard despite its having been (1) thrown out of the musical for which it had been written (Lady, Be Good! in 1924); (2) sung in a show that flopped on the road (the 1927 Strike Up the Band); (3) added and then cut from a third musical (Rosalie); and (4) rejected when Strike Up the Band was successfully revised in 1929. The reason for the last situation was ironic: the song had become too well known!

Words by Ira Gershwin **Music by George Gershwin**

Slowly, with expression

Pedal tacet

Some-day he'll come a-long, The Man I Love;

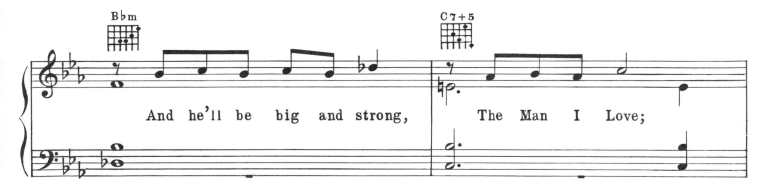

And he'll be big and strong, The Man I Love;

Embraceable You

Though written in 1928 for an unproduced operetta called East Is West, the Gershwin brothers' "Embraceable You" was not sung in public until two years later when 19-year-old Ginger Rogers did the honors in Girl Crazy. Note the way brother Ira managed to write three sets of four-syllable rhymes in a slow-tempo ballad without jarring the romantic mood so beautifully set by brother George.

Words by Ira Gershwin   **Music by George Gershwin**

'S Wonderful

Here lyricist Gershwin's aim was to achieve the amusingly sibilant sound caused by dropping the "it" from the contraction "it's," and slurring the remaining "s" as part of the following word. The result: 's lovely to play and 's fun to sing. Fred Astaire's sister, Adele, first introduced the song in the 1927 musical Funny Face.

Words by Ira Gershwin

Music by George Gershwin

Someone to Watch Over Me

When forlorn Gertrude Lawrence, clutching a rag doll, sang this gentle plea in the 1926 musical Oh, Kay!, a Broadway critic confessed that the Gershwins had "wrung the withers of even the most hard-hearted of those present." Composer George had originally written the melody in uptempo but soon realized that it sounded far better as a slow romantic ballad.

Words by Ira Gershwin   **Music by George Gershwin**

Fascinating Rhythm

"Fascinating" is the proper term for this combination of words and music. After receiving the melody from his brother, lyricist Gershwin faced an enormous task: the jagged, syncopated tune with its tricky accents hardly lent itself to a boy-girl expression, either amorous or humorous. So he simply hit upon a lyric describing the effects of a nagging, insinuating, fascinating rhythm. Fred and Adele Astaire first sang about it in the 1924 Broadway musical Lady, Be Good!

Words by
Ira Gershwin

Music by
George Gershwin

Fas - ci - nat - ing Rhy - thm, You've got me on the go! Fas - ci - nat - ing Rhy - thm, I'm all a -

✳ Performing note: Keep the right hand in a fixed position on this and similar passages.

Night and Day

"Night and Day" was created to fit the limited singing range of Fred Astaire, who introduced it in the 1932 musical Gay Divorce. As a lyricist, Cole Porter showed his great skill at depicting opposites: "night and day," "near or far," "traffic's boom" and "lonely room." As a melodist, he composed a compelling theme spun out to 16 bars, repeated, and brought back, somewhat abridged, within the final eight.

Words and Music by Cole Porter

Moderate Latin tempo

mf

Night And Day___

D♭maj7   C7   Fmaj9   F6

you are the   one, _____   On - ly you___

D♭maj7   C7   Fmaj9   F6

___ be - neath the   moon and un - der the   sun. _____   Wheth - er

What Is
This Thing Called Love?

It was while listening to native chants in Marrakesh, Morocco, that Cole Porter got the inspiration for this dark, brooding melody of despair. Introduced in London in the 1929 revue Wake Up and Dream!, *the song became so well known that by the time the show was brought over to New York the following year audiences greeted it as an old favorite.*

Words and Music by Cole Porter

To get into the proper creative mood for his 1935 Broadway musical Jubilee, *Cole Porter hied himself off on an around-the-world cruise. Many exotic locales obligingly furnished the inspiration for some of his creations, most notably the Indonesian island of Kalabahi where a native war dance inspired the theme for "Begin the Beguine," once described by* Time *magazine as being "structured as artfully as a classical sonata, the theme elaborated and subtly expanded each time it returns, developed until it finally crests and crashes. . . ."*

Words and Music by Cole Porter

Begin the Beguine

brings back a night _____ of trop - i - cal splen - dour, _____ It

brings back a mem - o - ry ev - er green. _____ I'm

with you once more _____ un - der the stars, _____ And

down by the shore _____ an or - ches - tra's play - ing, _____ And

e - ven the palms _____ seem to be sway - ing _____

mo-ments di-vine, ____ what rap-ture se - rene, ____ Till

clouds came a-long to dis-perse the joys we had tast - ed, ____ And

now when I hear peo-ple curse the chance that was wast - ed, ____ I

know but too well ____ what they mean; So don't

let them Be-gin ____ The Be-guine, ____ Let the

love that was once a-fire re-main an em - ber; _____ Let it

sleep like the dead de - sire I on-ly re-mem - ber _____

When they Be-gin _____ The Be - guine. _____ Oh yes,

let them Be-gin The Be - guine, make them play _____ Till the

stars that were there be-fore re-turn a - bove you, _____ Till you

You Do Something to Me

The release, or middle part, of a standard popular song has seldom been more excitingly constructed than in "You Do Something to Me." Here the melody seems to take wings on a flight of pure ecstasy as it punches out the message with those infectious interior rhymes: "Do do that voo *doo that* you *do so well." The song, a product of 1929, was introduced in Cole Porter's first Broadway success,* Fifty Million Frenchmen.

Words and Music by Cole Porter

Moderately

p (Quasi Tom-Tom)

You Do Some-thing To Me, Some-thing that sim-ply mys-ti - fies me.

mp Tell me, why it should be You have the

83

I Get a Kick Out of You

Words and Music by Cole Porter

Cole Porter's lighthearted but basically torchy ballad at first appears to fall into the familiar A-A-B-A pattern, with each section consisting of 16 bars. Yet both times the "A" theme is repeated, only the first six bars remain constant, the rest indulging in some compelling variations. This is particularly true in the final section in which the tones rise higher and higher with the plane's ascent, only to descend as the words express total indifference to the flight. "I Get a Kick Out of You" was first sung in 1934 by Ethel Merman in the musical Anything Goes.

My Heart Stood Still

No lyric writer has ever enjoyed a greater reputation for intricate, polysyllabic rhyming than Lorenz Hart. Yet Hart could also be both eloquent and simple, which he proved conclusively in his words for "My Heart Stood Still." Here not only do we get so meaningful a line as "That unfelt clasp of hands," but the entire lyric—with the exception of just six words—was put together with words of only one syllable. First sung in a London revue in 1927, the ballad was later heard in the Broadway musical A Connecticut Yankee.

Words by Lorenz Hart

Music by Richard Rodgers

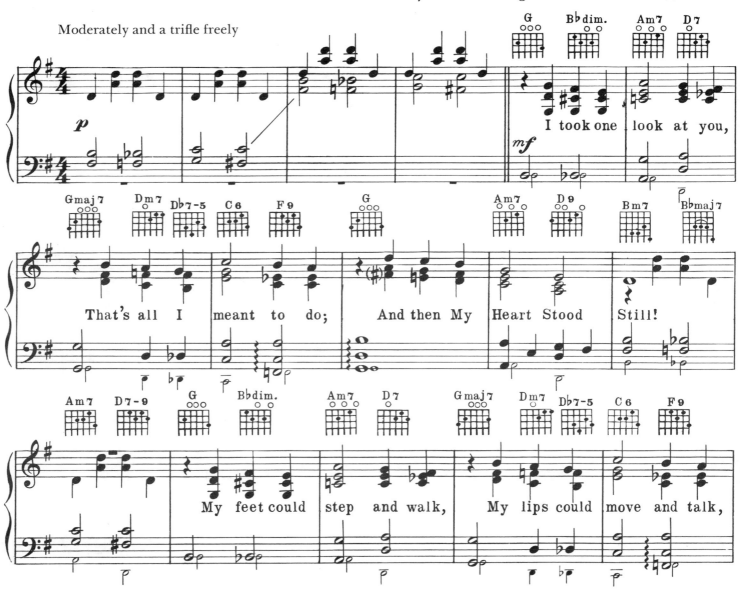

Thou Swell

Words by
Lorenz Hart

Music by
Richard Rodgers

The mating of Olde Englishe with 1927 slang was accomplished with great style in Rodgers and Hart's "Thou Swell." Surprisingly, when first sung in A Connecticut Yankee *during the show's Philadelphia tryout, the number left audiences so cold that the producer wanted it taken out of the score. Rodgers fought to keep it in and won vindication when it became one of the musical's most durable treasures.*

Moderately, with a bounce

Dancing on the Ceiling

Had Florenz Ziegfeld not taken such a strong dislike to "Dancing on the Ceiling," the song would have been unveiled in his Broadway musical Simple Simon, *early in 1930. But Rodgers and Hart didn't have long to wait for a spot to be found for it in their next musical,* Ever Green, *which opened in London later the same year. Sung by Jessie Matthews, the lilting air became the showstopper of the production.*

Words by Lorenz Hart   Music by Richard Rodgers

He danc-es o-ver-head On the ceil-ing, near my bed, In my sight, Through the night. I try to hide in vain

With a Song in My Heart

The appearance of movie star Glenn Hunter in the 1929 musical Spring Is Here presented a problem: he couldn't sing. Unfazed, Rodgers and Hart gave "With a Song in My Heart" to his more vocally gifted "rival," John Hundley.

Words by Lorenz Hart
Music by Richard Rodgers

Slowly, but rhythmically

With A Song In My Heart I be-hold your a - dor - a - ble face.

Just a song at the start, But it soon is a hymn to your grace.

When the mu - sic swells I'm touch-ing your hand;

The Blue Room

Words by
Lorenz Hart

Music by
Richard Rodgers

This tender ode to domestic tranquility was first sung in the 1926 musical
The Girl Friend. *Note how skillfully the key word "room" is emphasized*
in the first and second eight-bar sections: Everytime it is sung it is preceded
by the rhyme falling on "C," with the word itself raised one tone higher.

Tea for Two

"A dummy lyric" is a temporary set of words put together to help lyricists work out a song's metric form and rhyme scheme. *"Tea for Two"* may be a classic, but it still uses the dummy lyric Caesar dashed off hurriedly one night. The cheerful number was added to the 1924 musical No, No, Nanette.

Words by Irving Caesar

Music by Vincent Youmans

Pic-ture you up-on my knee, Just Tea For Two and two for tea, Just me for you and you for me a-lone. _____ No-bod-y near us to see us or hear us, No friends or re-la-tions on week-end va-ca-tions, We won't have it known, dear, that

98

You and the Night and the Music

This smoldering confession was first uttered by Libby Holman in the 1934 musical Revenge with Music. *Although it won acclaim on Broadway, radio censors frowned on the line, "fill me with flaming desire," and barred the song from the air.*

Words by Howard Dietz
Music by Arthur Schwartz

101

Something to Remember You By

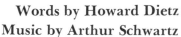

When first sung in a 1929 London musical, this melody had a snappy beat and was mated to a comic verse called "I Have No Words." Later, lyricist Dietz came up with the present title and composer Schwartz slowed down the melody.

Words by Howard Dietz
Music by Arthur Schwartz

Smoothly and rhythmically

Oh, give me Some-thing To Re-mem-ber You By,

When you are far a-way from me, dear.

Some lit-tle some-thing mean-ing love can-not die,

103

Dancing in the Dark

"Dancing in the Dark" was a product of sheer inspiration. While working on the score for the 1931 Broadway revue The Band Wagon, *composer Schwartz was groping for—in his words—"a dark song, somewhat mystical, yet in slow, even rhythm." For days nothing would satisfy him. Then one morning he awoke with this melody so fixed in his head that all he had to do was jot down the notes.*

Words by
Howard Dietz

Music by
Arthur Schwartz

Danc - ing In The Dark ___ Till the tune ends, We're

Danc - ing In The Dark ___ And it soon ends; We're

waltz - ing in the won - der of why we're here.

Mack the Knife

In 1928 in Berlin, on the day before the dress rehearsal of his new work, Die Dreigroschenoper, *Kurt Weill became convinced that an additional song was needed to provide thematic unity to the story. Overnight he and collaborator Brecht devised a 64-bar piece consisting of two eight-bar themes, each one repeated three times, in imitation of a ghoulish form of 17th-century ballad called a Moritat (literally, "murder deed"). Though the song became popular throughout Europe, it wasn't until 1952, in Marc Blitzstein's English version, that both* The Threepenny Opera *and its theme, "Mack the Knife," found a receptive public in the United States.*

German words by Bertolt Brecht   **Music by Kurt Weill**   **English lyrics by Marc Blitzstein**

Moderato, with a beat

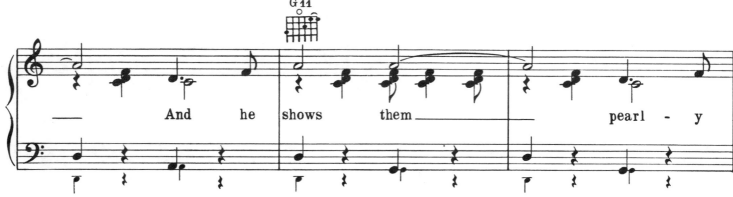

When the shark bites with his teeth, dear,
Scarlet billows start to spread.
Fancy gloves, though, wears MacHeath, dear,
So there's not a trace of red.

From a tugboat by the river
A cement bag's dropping down;
The cement's just for the weight, dear,
Bet you Mackie's back in town.

On the sidewalk Sunday morning
Lies a body oozing life;
Someone's sneaking 'round the corner.
Is the someone Mack the Knife?

Louie Miller disappeared, dear,
After drawing out his cash;
And MacHeath spends like a sailor.
Did our boy do something rash?

Sukey Tawdry, Jenny Diver,
Polly Peachum, Lucy Brown,
Oh, the line forms on the right, dear,
Now that Mackie's back in town.

April in Paris

Words by E. Y. Harburg   **Music by Vernon Duke**

"Oh, to be in Paris now that April's here!" boomed a nostalgic Monty Woolley at a Manhattan bistro one day in 1932. "April in Paris," announced composer Vernon Duke dramatically. "What a title!" And he promptly composed this lovely song.

109

The Birth of the Blues

**Words by
B. G. DeSylva and Lew Brown**

Music by Ray Henderson

In the 1926 edition of the George White's Scandals, the first-act finale depicted a blues-vs-classics battle. The issue: whether the blues were worthy to enter musical Valhalla. When Harry Richman related the genesis of the musical form via "The Birth of the Blues," those in charge became convinced of the music's worth, the gates opened, and the curtain fell on a glimpse of indigo-spotlighted angels trilling the final notes.

Moderate blues tempo
No Chord

They heard the breeze in the trees Sing-ing weird mel-o-dies, And they made that The start of the blues.

(No Chord) And from a jail came the wail Of a down-heart-ed frail, And they played that As part of the blues.

I'm Just Wild About Harry

A musical comedy called Shuffle Along *came down from Harlem in 1921 to become the first all-Negro production ever to achieve a lengthy run on Broadway, thus setting the vogue for many such attractions in the 1920s. Among the ragtime pleasures was the strutting "I'm Just Wild About Harry," whose irresistible beat and easy-to-remember words have kept it an all-time favorite.*

Words and Music by Noble Sissle and Eubie Blake

of his kiss - es Fill me with ec - sta - sy. He's

sweet just like ___ choc'-late can - dy, And just like hon -

- ey from the bee. ___ Oh, I'm Just Wild ___ A - bout

Har - ry And he's just wild ___ a - bout, can - not do

___ with - out, He's just wild ___ a-bout me.

I'll See You Again

Noel Coward's operetta Bitter Sweet *(London, 1929) offered the touching romance between a Victorian English girl and her Viennese music teacher whom she marries and who is later killed in a duel. The recurring waltz theme, "I'll See You Again," which, according to Coward, "just dropped into my head, whole and complete" during a taxi ride, was first sung in the guise of a musical exercise by the hero and heroine.*

Words and Music by Noel Coward

Moderate waltz

I'll See You A - gain When - ev - er spring breaks through a - gain. Time may lie heav - y be-

Body and Soul

**Music by
John Green**

*Radio, sensitive in 1930, refused to allow this song on
the air because of its suggestive ending, so a new lyric
was written, with the last line laundered to "My castles
have crumbled, but I am his, body and soul."*

**Words by
Robert Sour,
Edward Heyman
and Frank Eyton**

Slowly, with expression

My heart is sad and lone-ly, For you I sigh, for you, dear, on-ly.

Why have-n't you seen it? I'm all for you, Bod-y And Soul!

I spend my days in long-ing And won-d'ring why it's me you're wrong-ing;

I tell you I mean it, I'm all for you Bod-y And Soul!

As Time Goes By

The line "Play it again, Sam" never fails to conjure up the scene in Casablanca in which Humphrey Bogart, drunk and despondent in his deserted café, listens as Dooley Wilson plays and croons the memory-evoking strains of "As Time Goes By." Though the film was released in 1942, the song had actually been introduced 11 years earlier by Frances Williams in a long-forgotten Broadway musical, Everybody's Welcome.

Words and Music by Herman Hupfeld

DAYS OF WINE AND ROSES

Not only an Academy Award winner, this evocative film theme also took home the "Grammy" honors of the recording industry as best song of 1962. Composer Mancini put his melody together from two nearly identical 16-bar sections, while lyricist Mercer matched this effort with a poignant, poetic message that managed to say all that was needed in exactly two sentences.

Words by Johnny Mercer   **Music by Henry Mancini**

Moderate ballad

mp

The Days _____ Of Wine And Ros - es _____

Laugh and run a - way _____ Like a child at play,

_____ Through the mead - ow - land to - ward a clos - ing door, A

door marked "Nev-er-more," That was-n't there be-fore. ___ The

lone - ly night dis-clos - es ___ Just a pass-ing breeze ___

___ Filled with mem-o-ries ___ Of the gold-en smile that in-tro-duced me

to ___ The Days Of Wine And Ros-es and

you. ___ *cresc.* *f* *rall.* *mp sub*

I Only Have Eyes for You

With the stars twinkling above and the island of Manhattan aglow in the distance, the poor young songwriter and his girl were seen snuggling against the rail of the Staten Island ferry. The hero was oblivious to everything but the heroine—a condition he expressed in song. And when he was finished, what did the misty-eyed girl say? "Gee, Jimmy, that was swell." It all took place on the silver screen in 1934: Dick Powell and Ruby Keeler in Dames.

Words by Al Dubin

Music by Harry Warren

Are the stars out to-night?___ I don't know if it's cloud-y or bright___ 'Cause I On-ly Have Eyes For You, dear.___ The moon may be high,___ but I can't see a thing in the sky, 'Cause I On-ly Have Eyes For You.

I don't know if we're in a gar - den,

Or on a crowd -ed av - e - nue. You _____ are here, so am I, _____ May -be mil-lions of peo -ple go by, _____ But they all dis -ap-pear _____ from view, _____ And I On - ly Have Eyes _____ For You. _____

Secret Love

Spurred by Broadway's hit musical western *Annie Get Your Gun*, Hollywood staked its own claim to similar sagebrush territory in *Calamity Jane. With Doris Day as the hoydenish heroine and Howard Keel as "Wild Bill" Hickok, the bang-up saga had all sorts of explosive numbers, but only one romantic piece, "Secret Love." The ballad became a 1953 Oscar-winner, a top-selling Doris Day recording and the most durable item in the score.*

Words by Paul Francis Webster
Music by Sammy Fain

Moderately, with tenderness

Once I had a Se-cret Love That lived with-in the heart of me. All too soon my Se-cret Love Be-came im-pa-tient to be free. So I told a friend-ly star, The way that dream-ers oft-en

do, _____ Just how won-der-ful you are, ____ And why I'm so in love with you. ____ Now I shout it from the high - est hills, E - ven told the gold - en daf - fo - dils; At last my heart's an o - pen door, ____ And my se-cret love's no se-cret an - y more.

Too Marvelous for Words

Could the dictionary be at a loss for words? The song's thoroughly smitten swain thinks so after searching in vain to find the "magical adjectives" to describe his beloved. The number emanated from a 1937 film called Ready, Willing and Able, *whose only other distinction was that it starred Ruby Keeler without Dick Powell.*

Words by Johnny Mercer

Music by Richard A. Whiting

MY OWN TRUE LOVE

Tara Theme

The epic film Gone with the Wind *could scarcely be called a musical. Yet, like so many screen dramas, it did have a background score, one that has proved equally as lasting as the movie itself. The score's main theme even achieved Hit Parade status in two different forms: in 1941 as an instrumental known as "Tara Theme," and 13 years later, with a lyric, as the impassioned declaration, "My Own True Love."*

Words by Mack David   Music by Max Steiner

Slowly and majestically

My Own True Love, My Own True Love, At last I've found you, My Own True Love. No lips but yours, No arms but yours Will ev - er

★ Tune lowest string ½ tone higher to F

128

IT'S MAGIC

No song was ever more important to a singer's career than "It's Magic" was to the career of Doris Day. In 1948 the former band singer was signed by Warner Brothers for her first starring role in Romance on the High Seas. Her debut inspired Cahn and Styne to fashion the song establishing her both as movie star and recording artist. It wasn't long before the ballad became even more well known than the film; as a consequence, when it was shown in England, the title of the film was changed to It's Magic.

Music by
Jule Styne

Words by
Sammy Cahn

You sigh, the song be-gins, you speak and I hear vi - o - lins, It's Mag - ic. The stars de-sert the skies and rush to nes-tle in your eyes, It's Mag - ic. With-out a gold - en wand or mys-tic charms, Fan - tas - tic things be - gin when I am in your arms.

When we walk hand in hand the world be-comes a won-der-land, It's

Mag - ic.

How else can I ex-plain those rain-bows when there is no rain, It's

Mag - ic.

Why do I tell my-self these things that

hap-pen are all real-ly true? When in my heart I know the

mag - ic is my love for you.

IT CAN'T BE WRONG

Max Steiner was the acknowledged dean of film background composers during the 1930s and '40s. His compelling theme for star-crossed lovers Bette Davis and Paul Henreid in Now, Voyager stirred so many hearts that, well after the film had been released, it was refashioned into a song with a suitably guilt-plagued lyric. The broad and beautiful melody was typical of the romantic sound Steiner put into all of the many Bette Davis films he scored.

Words by Kim Gannon

Music by Max Steiner

Lulu's Back in Town

Minus dancing girls or Busby Berkeley spectacles, the 1935 movie musical Broadway Gondolier *had only a slender plot line about a radio crooner (Dick Powell) upon which to string along a collection of engaging tunes. This one tells of the impecunious Mr. Otis gaily preening for his date with the long-absent Lulu.*

Words by Al Dubin
Music by Harry Warren

Moderately, with a jazz feel

Got-ta get my old tux-e-do pressed,— Got-ta sew a but-ton on my vest,— 'Cause to-night I've got-ta look my best, Lu-lu's Back In Town. Got-ta get a half-a-buck some-where,— Got-ta shine my shoes and slick my hair,— Got-ta get my-self a

Blues in the Night

Words by Johnny Mercer

Written for a film called Hot Nocturne, *this song became so popular that the picture was retitled* Blues in the Night.

Music by Harold Arlen

wor-ri-some thing who'll leave ya t' sing the Blues _____ In The Night.

Now the rain's a fall-in', Hear the train a-call-in', Whoo-ee, ___ (My ma-ma done tol' me, ___)

Hear that lone-some whis-tle Blow-in' 'cross the tres-tle, Whoo-ee, ___ (My ma-ma done tol' me, ___) A

whoo-ee-duh whoo-ee, ___ Ol' click-e-ty clack's a-ech-o-in' back th' Blues _____ In The Night. (Hum

_____) My ma-ma was right, there's Blues In The Night. _____

You Must Have Been a Beautiful Baby

"You Must Have Been a Beautiful Baby" was first sung by Dick Powell to Olivia De Havilland in an all-but-forgotten epic of 1938 called Hard to Get. *A musically compact song with an engaging offbeat construction, it also benefited from lyricist Mercer's unique notion of romancing a girl by imagining how beautiful she had been as a child.*

Words by Johnny Mercer   Music by Harry Warren

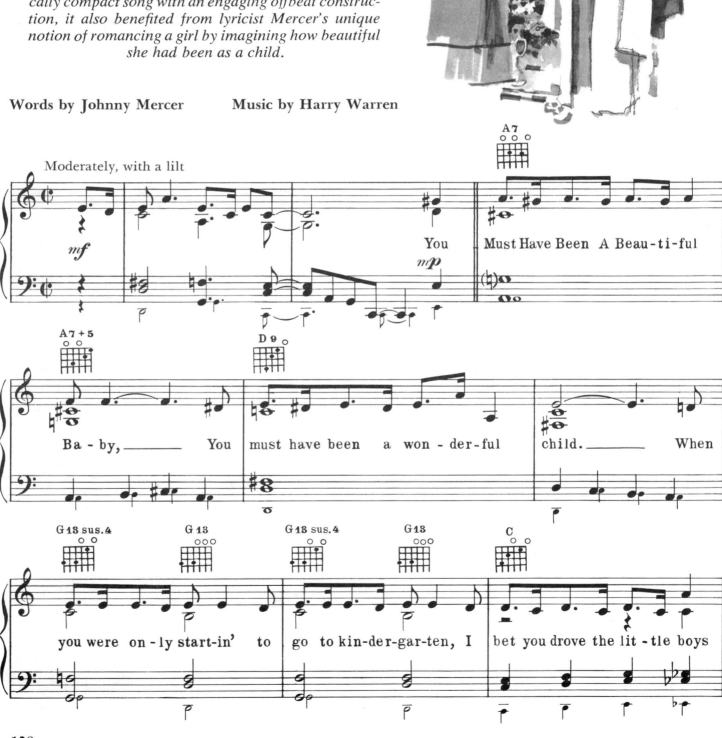

Moderately, with a lilt

mf   *mp*

You Must Have Been A Beau-ti-ful Ba - by, ___ You must have been a won-der-ful child. ___ When you were on - ly start-in' to go to kin-der-gar-ten, I bet you drove the lit - tle boys

wild.   And   when it came to win-ning blue   rib-bons, _____   You

must have shown the oth-er kids   how.   I can see the judg-es'eyes as they

hand-ed you   the prize, I   bet you made the cut-est   bow,   Oh! You

Must Have Been A Beau-ti-ful   Ba - by, ___ 'Cause ba-by look   at you

now.

cresc.

f

p cresc.

(No Chord)

ff

139

Jeepers Creepers

In "Jeepers Creepers" lyricist Mercer put together a lyric based primarily on a collection of teen-age slang of the '30s, including the rhyming of "jeepers creepers" with "peepers" and "weepers," and "heaters" with "cheaters." This swinging tribute to a young lady's ocular attractions was written especially for Louis Armstrong, whose mellow growl presented it first on the screen in Going Places and then on a best-selling record.

**Words by Johnny Mercer
Music by Harry Warren**

Jeep - ers Creep - ers! Where'd ya get those peep - ers?__ Jeep - ers Creep - ers! Where'd ya get those eyes?

Gosh all git up! How'd they get so lit up?__

September in the Rain

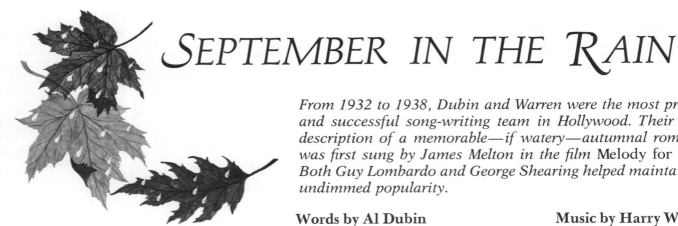

From 1932 to 1938, Dubin and Warren were the most prolific and successful song-writing team in Hollywood. Their fond description of a memorable—if watery—autumnal romance was first sung by James Melton in the film Melody for Two. *Both Guy Lombardo and George Shearing helped maintain its undimmed popularity.*

Words by Al Dubin   **Music by Harry Warren**

leaves of brown came tum-bling down, re-mem-ber?___ In Sep-
tem - ber, ___ In The Rain, ___ The
sun went out just like a dy-ing em - ber, ___ That Sep-

Bei Mir Bist Du Schön
[*Means that You're Grand*]

"Bei Mir Bist Du Schön" was a Yiddish song discovered in Harlem and made famous by three girls from Minneapolis. After hearing it belted out by a Negro trio at the Apollo Theater, Sammy Cahn became so excited about the number that he persuaded the Andrews Sisters to record it — even though they had no idea what the words meant. It was only when the record company insisted on an English lyric that Cahn and partner Chaplin batted out the appropriate lines.

Original lyrics by Jacob Jacobs
English version by Sammy Cahn and Saul Chaplin
Music by Sholom Secunda

-gain I'll ex- plain, *Boy:* It means you're the fair- est in the land.
Girl: It means that my heart's at your com - mand.

I could say "Bel - la, bel - la," ev - en say "Voon-der - bar," Each lan-guage

on - ly helps me tell you how grand you are. I've

tried to ex - plain Bei Mir Bist Du Schön, So kiss me and

say you un-der - stand.

IT HAD TO BE YOU

Although bandleader-composer Jones wrote this perennial hit with Gus Kahn in 1924, it became a "current" hit again in 1944 after appearing in the Eddie Cantor–George Murphy movie Show Business. *There was a ban on new recording that year, but RCA reissued an Earl Hines recording that had been made in 1941, and it became a bestseller. The song has been used in no less than 40 feature-length films plus dozens of shorts!*

Words by Gus Kahn　　　　　**Music by Isham Jones**

It Had To Be You, It Had To Be You, I wan-dered a-round and fin-al-ly found the some-bod-y who Could make me be true, could make me be blue, And e-ven be

glad, just to be sad, think-ing of you. _____ Some oth-ers I've seen _____ might nev-er be mean, _____ Might nev-er be cross or try to be boss, but they would-n't do. _____ For no-bod-y else gave me a thrill, With all your faults I love you still, It Had To Be You, won-der-ful you, had to be you.

What's New?

In 1938, Bob Haggart, the bassist in Bob Crosby's orchestra, composed a soaring instrumental piece called "I'm Free," which spotlighted the band's trumpeter, Billy Butterfield. Its success prompted lyricist Burke to give it words and rename it "What's New?" Note that the third eight-bar section repeats the basic melody in a higher key.

Words by Johnny Burke

Music by Bob Haggart

149

When My Dream Boat Comes Home

In "When My Dream Boat Comes Home," Messrs. Franklin and Friend created an especially seaworthy ballad out of a familiar bugle call pattern, and then turned it over to Guy Lombardo to steer lovingly over the starlit waters. During the 1930s the authors wrote such well-remembered items as "The Merry-Go-Round Broke Down" and "You Can't Stop Me from Dreaming."

Words by Dave Franklin
Music by Cliff Friend

Moderately, with a bounce

When My Dream Boat Comes Home, Then my dreams no more will roam.

I will meet you and greet you,

*Boogit!**

* For easier version, play downbeats only   *etc.*

I Found a Million Dollar Baby

In 1932, using "million dollar" as an adjective in singing about one's beloved—and then putting her in the lowly surroundings of a five and ten cent store—was the kind of contrasting that could be well appreciated by a country caught in the grips of the Depression. First sung by Fanny Brice and other principals in the revue Crazy Quilt, *the jaunty piece was later interpolated in the movie* Million Dollar Baby.

Words by Billy Rose and Mort Dixon
Music by Harry Warren

It was a luck-y A-pril show-er, It was the most con-ven-ient door; I Found A Mil-lion Dol-lar Ba-by In a five and ten cent store; The rain con-tin-ued for an hour,— I hung a-round for three or four, A-round a mil-lion dol-lar

baby____ In a five and ten cent store. She was sell-ing chi - na
swing out a bit

____ and when she made those eyes _____ I kept buy-ing chi - na

____ un-til the crowd got wise. _____ In - ci-dent'-ly, if you should run in-to a

show-er, Just step in-side my cot-tage door And meet the mil-lion dol-lar

ba - by ____ From the five and ten cent store!

153

Heaven Can Wait

The "you've-made-a-heaven-for-me-on-earth" theme, a longtime favorite with popular-song poets, was given a new twist in this affectionate vow of fidelity. Here the singer even anticipates entering the realm of heaven with his beloved. With Jack Leonard on the vocal, Tommy Dorsey's orchestra introduced the ballad in 1939, and it remained high on the Hit Parade popularity charts for 11 weeks.

Words by Eddie DeLange   **Music by James Van Heusen**

You Go to My Head

Little wonder that it took this song some two years before finding a publisher in 1938. Radio at that time had a strict ruling against any reference to an alcoholic beverage and here was a lyric dealing with the heady effects of no less than three! The ballad was closely identified with the big bands of Glen Gray, Larry Clinton and Mitchell Ayres.

Words by Haven Gillespie   Music by J. Fred Coots

157

KISS ME AGAIN

Fifi, the leading character in Victor Herbert's frothy operetta Mlle. Modiste, *works for a Parisian milliner but dreams of someday becoming an actress. To demonstrate her theatrical versatility, she devises a lengthy routine called* If I Were on the Stage *in which she attempts three different types of songs. First there is a gavotte for a country maid, second a polonaise for a lady of history. To introduce her final selection, she explains that her favorite role would be "emotional and full of soul" and glides into the sensuous waltz "Kiss Me Again."*

Words by Henry Blossom   **Music by Victor Herbert**

Gypsy Love Song

Words by Harry B. Smith
Music by Victor Herbert

Victor Herbert, the most celebrated composer of operetta America has ever known, wrote the musical scores for no less than 41 productions. The Fortune Teller, presented in 1898, featured "Gypsy Love Song."

Slum-ber on, my lit-tle gyp-sy sweet-heart, Dream of the field and the grove. Can you hear me, hear me in that dream-land, Where your fan - cies rove? Slum - ber on, my lit-tle gyp-sy sweet-heart, Wild lit-tle wood-land dove. Can you hear the song that tells you All my - heart's true love?

I'm Falling in Love with Someone

By the middle of the second act of Victor Herbert's Naughty Marietta, *it is obvious to all that the friendship between Captain Dick Warrington and Marietta D'Altena has ripened into a far stronger emotion, a condition our hero fervently reveals in the beautiful, soaring "I'm Falling in Love with Someone." Note the composer's daring leap of a ninth in order to accentuate those all-important words "one girl" (and later "to see").*

Words by Rida Johnson Young
Music by Victor Herbert

Ah! Sweet Mystery of Life

The Victor Herbert score for Naughty Marietta *is universally accepted as his greatest, topped by the cascading duet "Ah! Sweet Mystery of Life." The song is used throughout the operetta as a*

romantic motif since the coquettish Marietta, unable to recall more than fragments of this mysterious "Dream Melody" (originally the alternate title), vows to give her heart only to the man who can complete it. No problem at all when it turns out to be none other than dashing Captain Dick.

Words by Rida Johnson Young
Music by Victor Herbert

hopes, the joy and i - dle tears that fall! For 'tis

love and love a - lone, the world is seek - ing; And 'tis

love, and love a - lone, that can re - pay! 'Tis the

an - swer, 'tis the end and all of liv - ing,_____ For it is

love a - lone that rules for aye!

165

Indian Summer

Words by
Al Dubin

Music by
Victor Herbert

Victor Herbert composed "Indian Summer" in 1919 as a piano piece subtitled "An American Idyll," and exactly 20 years later lyricist Dubin furnished the words that turned it into a song. "It was particularly difficult," Dubin once said, "because I couldn't change even one note of a melody that was never intended to be sung. It took me two weeks to finish it."

Stouthearted Men

A well-nigh irresistible recruiting call for stout-voiced singers, "Stouthearted Men" performs a similar function for a male chorus of bond servants in the operetta The New Moon. *Through the first 12 bars the leading baritone makes his lofty appeal in a thumping march rhythm; then, with the men primed and ready, he rallies them in two-four time to a vision of what so valorous a group might achieve. In the musical, at least, it's quite a lot. The men stage a mutiny aboard the good ship* New Moon *and sail away to a Caribbean island where they set up their own colony.*

Words by Oscar Hammerstein II   **Music by Sigmund Romberg**

soon give you ten thou-sand more, Oh! Shoul-der to shoul-der and

bold - er and bold-er they grow as they go to the fore!

Then _____ there's noth-ing in the world can halt or

mar a plan, _____ When _____ Stout-heart-ed

Men _____ can stick to-geth-er man to man!

Lover, Come Back to Me

The New Moon, *a Hammerstein-Romberg operetta of 1928, was one of the few musicals ever to close down completely and then, rewritten and restaged, become a standing-room-only attraction on Broadway. Unquestionably, much of the credit must go to the songs that were added, including the burning, yearning "Lover, Come Back to Me," sung by the show's prima donna, Evelyn Herbert.*

Words by Oscar Hammerstein II   Music by Sigmund Romberg

The sky was blue, And high a-bove The moon was new And so was love.

This eag-er heart of mine was sing - ing: "Lov-er, where can you be?"

You came at last, Love had its day, That day is past, You've gone a-way.

ONE ALONE

That stirring vow of fidelity, "One Alone," from The Desert Song, *is part of a three-way musical discussion called "Eastern and Western Love." Representing the "eastern" points of view, one Moroccan tribesman advises treating love as a passing pleasure, while another advocates a "harem of blossoms." But the Red Shadow, a Frenchman in disguise, rejects both ideas. He pledges his undying devotion to "one alone to be my own."*

Words by Otto Harbach and Oscar Hammerstein II
Music by Sigmund Romberg

SERENADE

Words by Dorothy Donnelly
Music by Sigmund Romberg

Although The Student Prince *had the longest Broadway run of any Sigmund Romberg operetta, its chances looked so bleak at the beginning of its out-of-town tryout that the producer insisted on making drastic changes. Among them, the elimination of "Serenade," Romberg's favorite song in the score. The composer, conceding other alterations, held firm on "Serenade," and it stayed in—only to receive the show's biggest ovation.*

O - ver-head the moon is beam - ing, White as blos-soms on the bough; Noth-ing is heard but the song of a bird,— Fill-ing all the air with dream-ing! Could my heart but still its beat - ing, On - ly you can tell it how, ——— Be-lov-ed! From your win-dow give me greet-ing, I swear my e-ter - nal love.

Jalousie

Jacob Gade was a Danish violinist who at one time was a member of the New York Symphony Orchestra. After returning to Copenhagen, he wrote, among other light compositions, a "Gypsy tango" called "Jalousie," which he published himself. Imported in 1931, the melody was outfitted with words by the daughter of New York Congressman Sol Bloom. Arthur Fiedler's recording with the Boston "Pops" Orchestra became the first "light classic" to reach a sale of one million records.

Words by Vera Bloom   **Music by Jacob Gade**

Jeal - ous - y, _____ Night and day you tor - ture me! _____ I some - times won - der, _____ If this spell that I'm un - der Can be on - ly a mel - o - dy, _____ For I know no one but me _____ Has won your

heart but, When the mu - sic starts, ___ My peace de -
parts from the mo - ment they play ___ that lan-gour-ous strain,
And we sur - ren - der to all ___ its charm once a - gain.
This jeal-ous - y That tor-tures me
Is ec-sta - sy, Mys-ter - y, pain!

175

We dance to a tan-go of love,_____
Your heart beats with mine as we sway.
Your eyes give the an-swer I'm dream-ing of,_____
That soft word your cruel lips will nev-er say!_____ I

fear that the mu - sic will end,

And shat - ter the spell it may

lend, To make me be -

lieve, When your eyes just de - ceive, And it's

on - ly the tan - go you love.

Yours Is My Heart Alone

Original text by Ludwig Herzer and Fritz Lohner
English version by Harry B. Smith
Music by Franz Lehár

Moderately, but not too fast

Yours Is My Heart A - lone_____ And with - out you life holds no charm; Yours ev - 'ry

In 1929, Viennese composer Franz Lehár's operetta **The Land of Smiles** *was a resounding hit for two main reasons: the aria, "Yours Is My Heart Alone," and the tenor voice of Richard Tauber to sing it. This rich, melodic outpouring occurs in the story soon after the leading character, a Chinese prince, has revealed to his Viennese bride that, according to custom, he must also take four Chinese wives. Insisting that this is a mere formality, he tries with desperate urgency to convince his beloved Lisa that his heart is for her alone.*

Love Sends a Little Gift of Roses

Words by Leslie Cooke

Music by John Openshaw

Slowly, with expression

Love Sends A Lit - tle Gift Of Ros - es,

Breath - ing a pray'r un - to my po - sies,

Torn from my heart as twi - light clos - es, Ask - ing this,

More than any other flower, the rose has flourished in the creative gardens of the world's foremost poets and melodists. It may be the yellow rose of Texas or a shining one in Picardy, that wild one in Ireland or the last of the summer. Yet no matter what color or origin, the rose is always something special as a fragrant symbol of love.

on - ly this, One heart to grow a lit - tle ten - der, Two eyes to glow with love's own splen - dour, Two lips to give in sweet sur - ren - der, Just a kiss, just a kiss.

In the Good Old Summertime

Words by Ren Shields

Music by George Evans

"There's nothing like the good old summertime," remarked minstrel headliner "Honeyboy" Evans while dining outdoors one evening in 1902. "Not a bad song title," responded partner Shields, who turned up with the completed lyric a few days later. Since Evans was musically untrained, he simply hummed his tune while a friend, singer Blanche Ring, took down the notes.

By the Light
of the Silvery Moon

Words by Edward Madden

Music by Gus Edwards

Apart from "beams" and "dreams," the entire rhyme scheme of the refrain describing this appealing summertime tryst is confined to the "oon" sound, possibly the most delightful example of rhyming frugality to be found. The number, long a barbershop quartet favorite, was introduced in 1909 by child singer Georgie Price, planted in theater audiences as part of Gus Edwards' vaudeville sketch School Boys and Girls. *Later the same year it helped brighten the Ziegfeld Follies.*

Love's Old Sweet Song

Little is known about the origin of this simple yet unforgettable song except that it was first published in London in 1884 and that its melody was created by an Irish barrister turned composer.

Words and Music by J. L. Molloy

Just a song at twi - light, when the lights are low; And the flick -'ring shad - ows soft - ly come and go, Tho' the heart be wear - y, sad the day and long, Still to us at twi - light comes love's old song, comes Love's_ Old Sweet_ Song.

Cuddle Up a Little Closer, Lovey Mine

Although this piece was originally created for a vaudeville act,
it was only when the writers didn't get paid that they added it
to the score of their first Broadway show, Three Twins.

Words by Otto Harbach
Music by Karl Joschna

There Is a Tavern in the Town

Originally "There Is a Tavern in the Town" had been a drinking ballad sung by ale-swigging miners of Cornwall, England, with the opening line, "There is an alehouse in our town." But it was first published in the United States in 1883 in a collection called Students' Songs. Ever since, it has been primarily identified with bibulous collegians.

Cornish Folk Song

laugh - ter____free, And nev - er, nev - er thinks of me.____ Fare thee

well, for I must leave thee, Do not let the part-ing grieve thee, And re-mem-ber that the best of friends must

part, must part. A - dieu, a-dieu kind friends a - dieu (Say a-dieu). I

can no long-er stay with you (Stay with you).__ I'll__ hang my harp on a

weep-ing wil-low tree, And may the world go well with thee._____

Hello! My Baby

While touring in vaudeville in 1899, Joe Howard overheard a Negro porter in a Scranton, Pennsylvania, hotel talk to his girl on the telephone. His conversation gave Howard the idea for his cake-walking, ragtime telephone number, "Hello! My Baby," which he wrote with his wife. Two weeks later Howard introduced it on stage to enthusiastic acclaim.

Words and Music by Joseph E. Howard and Ida Emerson

Hel-lo! My Ba-by, hel-lo! my hon-ey, hel-lo! my rag-time gal; Send me a kiss by wire, ba-by my heart's on fire! If you re-fuse me, hon-ey, you'll lose me, then you'll be left a-lone. Oh, ba-by, tel-e-phone and tell me I'm your own.

Young Jimmy Walker, later mayor of New York, scribbled the title of this song on a piece of paper and handed it to composer Ball. The latter encouraged Walker to complete the lyric — a none too taxing chore since the title took up about half the words in the refrain.

Will You Love Me in December as You Do in May?

Words by James J. Walker   **Music by Ernest R. Ball**

In the Shade of the Old Apple Tree

Two struggling songwriters were ambling through New York's Central Park one sunny day in 1905. Their inability to find even one apple tree started them longing for their midwestern boyhood homes so bountiful with apple trees. Sufficiently inspired, they dashed back to the publishing firm for which they worked and created their timeless ode to the simple joys of country living.

Words by Harry Williams   **Music by Egbert Van Alstyne**

Slow waltz

In The Shade Of The Old Ap - ple Tree, ___ Where the love in your eyes I could see; ___ When the voice that I heard, Like the

In My Merry Oldsmobile

Words by Vincent Bryan
Music by Gus Edwards

Gay waltz tempo

Come a-way with me Lu-cile, In My Mer-ry Olds-mo-bile, Down the road of life we'll fly

Transportation songs were clogging the market during the century's first two decades, but few managed to achieve the musical mileage of the rollicking waltz "In My Merry Oldsmobile." Inspiration was supplied by a well-publicized trip made in 1905 by two Oldsmobiles. It took them 44 days to make their way from Detroit to Portland, Oregon, thus marking the first cross-continent journey ever accomplished by automobile.

The Band Played On

Words by John F. Palmer
Music by Charles B. Ward

Bright waltz

Ca - sey would waltz with a straw-ber - ry blonde, And The Band Played On. ___ He'd glide cross the floor with the girl he a - dor'd, And The Band

One morning in the late 1800s, John Palmer, a young actor, was listening to a German street band outside his window. Distracted by sister Pauline's call to breakfast, he cried out dramatically, "One moment. Let the band play on." Pauline's comment — need it be noted? — was, "That's a good title for a song." Suitably goaded, Palmer penned the now legendary musical tale. However, he was unable to find a publisher until years later when vaudevillian Charles Ward expressed interest. Ward also made some minor alterations, thus giving him the excuse to take solo credit as composer.

I'll Take You Home Again, Kathleen

Contrary to a common misconception, this was not a ballad imported from the Emerald Isle. In 1876, composer Westendorf, a school teacher living in Plainfield, Indiana, penned this affectionate love song when temporarily separated from his wife—only her name was Jennie. The piece was written in the form of an "answer" to a then popular ballad, "Barney, Take Me Home Again."

Words and Music by Thomas P. Westendorf

Slowly, with expression

I'll Take You Home A-gain, Kath-leen, A-cross the o-cean wild and wide To where your heart has ev-er been Since first you were my bon-ny

bride. The ros - es all have left your cheek, I've watched them fade a - way and die. Your voice is sad when - e'er you speak And tears be-dim your lov - ing eyes. Oh, I will take you back, Kath- leen, To where your heart will feel no pain, And when the fields are fresh and green, I'll take you to your home, Kath- leen.

My Wild Irish Rose

Chauncey Olcott, the leading American-born Irish tenor at the turn of the century, won his fame primarily as the star of a series of sentimental plays about the old sod which were always embellished by at least five suitably Celtic airs. The perennially blooming "My Wild Irish Rose," from A Romance in Athlone *(1899), became the first Irish-flavored song success to emanate from a Broadway show.*

Words and Music by Chauncey Olcott

★ **Melody may be doubled an 8ᵛᵃ higher.**

none can com-pare With My Wild I - rish Rose.____

____ My Wild I - rish Rose,____ The

dear - est flow'r that grows,____ And some

day for my sake, She may let me take The

bloom from My Wild I - rish Rose.____

Once composer Ball discovered early in his career that he had a special gift for creating heart-tugging ballads, he never risked writing anything else. "People like songs they can take home to themselves," he said, and obliged by turning out such durable take-home pieces as "Will You Love Me in December as You Do in May?," "Mother Machree," "A Little Bit of Heaven" and "Love Me and the World Is Mine." Ball's lilting favorite, "When Irish Eyes Are Smiling," was first sung by the popular singing actor Chauncey Olcott, in the 1912 musical play The Isle o' Dreams.

When Irish Eyes Are Smiling

Words by Chauncey Olcott and George Graff, Jr.

Music by Ernest R. Ball

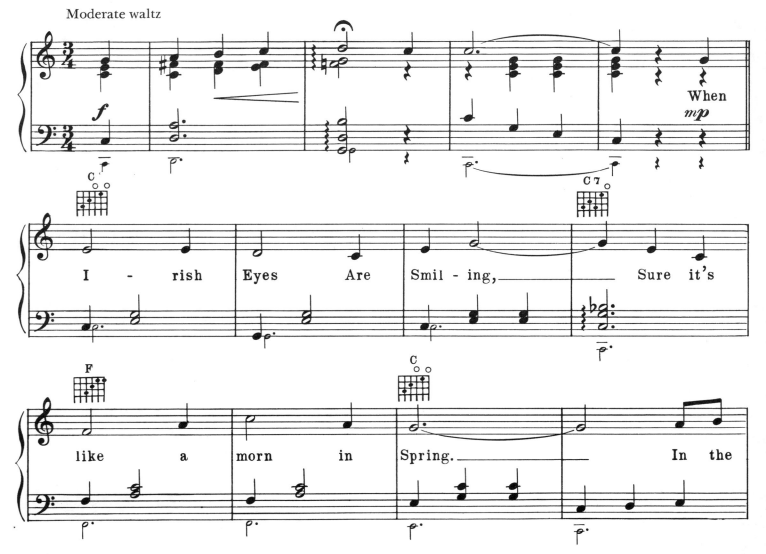

lilt of I - rish laugh-ter You can hear the an - gels sing. When I - rish hearts are hap - py, All the world seems bright and gay, And when I - rish Eyes Are Smil - ing, Sure they steal your heart a - way.

rall. *cresc.* *ten.*

That's an Irish Lullaby

It was in the 1914 play Shameen Dhu *(Gaelic for "Black Jamie") that Chauncey Olcott introduced this touching air. Modern audiences are more likely to associate it with the too-ra-loo-ra-loo-ral-ing of Bing Crosby in* Going My Way.

Words and Music by J. R. Shannon

Put on Your Old Grey Bonnet

Words by Stanley Murphy

Originally called "Put on Your Old Sunbonnet," this Wenrich-Murphy song, which sold over a million copies of sheet music, was renamed after the publisher had mistakenly substituted "grey" for "sun" in singing the first line.

Music by Percy Wenrich

Put On Your Old Grey Bon-net with the blue rib-bon on it, While I hitch old Dob-bin to the shay, ___ And through the fields of clo-ver, We'll drive up to Do-ver on our gold-en wed-ding day. ___

Memories

The career of composer Van Alstyne parallels that of many song-writers during the early days of the century: musical prodigy, vaudeville pianist, staff pianist for a New York publishing house, then, after years of struggling, eventual success. A decade after his first hit, "In the Shade of the Old Apple Tree," Van Alstyne created another timeless masterpiece, "Memories," one of his first works to be written with lyricist Kahn.

Words by Gus Kahn   **Music by Egbert Van Alstyne**

Moderate waltz

Mem - o - ries,   Mem - o - ries,

Dreams   of   love   so   true._____

Yankee Doodle Dandy

For his grand entrance as star of his own show, Little Johnny Jones, *George M. Cohan got off to a prancing, flag-waving start with "Yankee Doodle Dandy," a syncopated march in two-four time ending with the strains of the original "Yankee Doodle" tune. Obviously fashioned to reflect Cohan's own personality as well as that of the character he played, the song quickly became the actor's musical trademark. Cohan may well have been a real-life nephew of his Uncle Sam, but he was not above strengthening that relationship by delaying his birthday from the third to the fourth of July.*

Words and Music by George M. Cohan

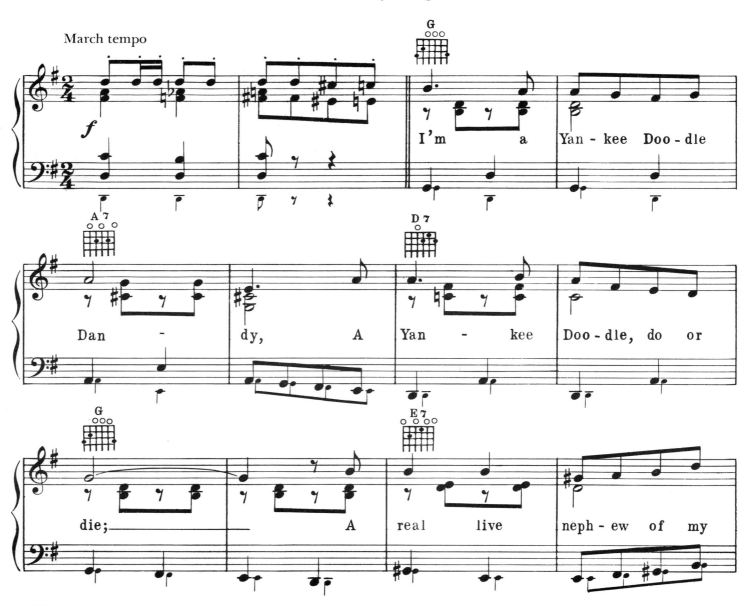

Oh, Promise Me

Had it not been for a show of temperament by actress Jessie Bartlett Davis, many of today's weddings might well be minus the majestic strains of "Oh, Promise Me." Following the Chicago premiere of Robin Hood *in 1890, Miss Davis, who played the male role of Alan-a-Dale, threatened to quit the company if she were not given a new aria which would show off her deep contralto tones. Desperate, composer De Koven recalled a piece he had written some time before, but which had never been sung in public. The actress rehearsed "Oh, Promise Me" the next day, sang it that night, and scored the biggest success of the production.*

Words by Clement Scott

Music by Reginald de Koven

Oh, Prom-ise Me, that some day you and I Will take our love to-geth-er to some sky Where we can be a-lone, and faith re -

I Love You Truly

Words and Music by Carrie Jacobs-Bond

Slowly

I Love You Truly, truly dear.

Life with its sor - rows,

After the tragic death of her husband, the need to earn a living obliged Carrie Jacobs-Bond to become a one-woman music business—composer, lyricist, publisher, song plugger and even sheet-music cover designer. Today her fame rests primarily on two songs, "I Love You Truly" and "A Perfect Day," both of which had to overcome initial public apathy before at last winning their rightful place in the nation's affection.

Black Is the Color

Many American folk songs, particularly those sung for generations in the southern Appalachian region, such as the wistful "Black Is the Color," have a marked kinship with the love songs of Elizabethan England.

American Folk Song

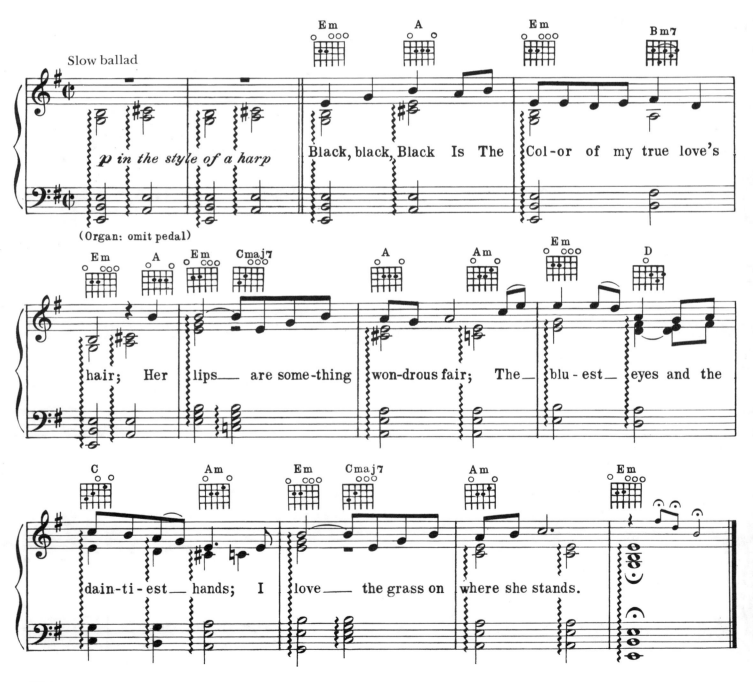

Greensleeves

The words of "Greensleeves" probably date back to 1580, but the music went un-published until the late 17th century. In The Merry Wives of Windsor *Shakespeare has Falstaff boom out, "Let the sky rain potatoes; let it thunder to the tune of 'Greensleeves.'"*

English Folk Song

Alas, my love,— you do me wrong__ To cast me off__ dis-cour-teous-ly, And
I have lov - ed you so long,__ De - light - ing in__ your com-pan-y.
Green-sleeves__was all my joy,__ Green - sleeves__was my de-light,
Green-sleeves was my heart of gold__ And who but my la - dy Green - sleeves.

Blowin' in the Wind

**Words and Music by
Bob Dylan**

Our current popular-music scene borrows heavily from the world of folk songs. Among modern balladeers, none has made a stronger impact than Bob Dylan, whose "Blowin' in the Wind," composed in 1962, practically became the anthem of the civil rights movement. The sensitive words, however, are equally applicable to any situation involving man's indifference to the basic rights of others. In 1964, Peter, Paul and Mary's recording of the song received "Grammy" awards both as the best performance by a vocal group and as the best folk song recording.

Brightly

How man-y roads must a man walk___ down Be- fore you call him a man?_____ Yes, 'n' how man-y seas must a white dove___

How many times must a man look up
Before he can see the sky?
Yes 'n' how many ears must one man have
Before he can hear people cry?
Yes 'n' how many deaths will it take till he knows
That too many people have died?
The answer my friend, is blowin' in the wind,
The answer is blowin' in the wind.

How many years can a mountain exist
Before it's washed to the sea?
Yes 'n' how many years can some people exist
Before they're allowed to be free?
Yes 'n' how many times can a man turn his head
Pretending he just doesn't see?
The answer my friend, is blowin' in the wind,
The answer is blowin' in the wind.

FOUR STRONG WINDS

Before Ian Tyson left his native British Columbia in the late 1950s, he had been a lumberjack, migrant farmworker, art student and rodeo rider. It was his experience as a seasonal farmhand that inspired this song. Written in 1963, "Four Strong Winds" was the first big hit for Ian and his former wife and singing partner Sylvia Fricker. "Many of these seasonal workers cross the country every year," explains Ian, "from the tobacco harvest in Ontario to apple picking in British Columbia. When the weather turns harsh, they must find a different type of work."

Words and Music by Ian Tyson

Moderately slow, but moving

Chorus

Four Strong Winds that blow lone-ly, Sev-en seas that run high, All those things that don't change come what may. But our good times are all gone And I'm

218

bound for mov-in' on, I'll look for you if I'm ev-er back this way. ___ I think I'll

go out to Al-ber-ta, Weath-er's good there in the fall; I got some friends that I can

go to work-in' for. ___ Still I wish you'd change your mind If I

asked you one more time, But we've been through that a hun-dred times or more. Repeat from %

If I get there before the snow flies
And if things are goin' good,
You could meet me if I sent you down the fare.
But by then it would be winter,
Ain't too much for you to do
And those winds sure can blow cold way out there.   (repeat Chorus till Fine)

Shenandoah

A short-haul chanty dearly loved by sailors on square-rigged ships,
"Shenandoah" tells of the love of a white man for the daughter of the
Indian chief after whom Virginia's Shenandoah Valley was named. The
song had originated as a land ballad sung by lumberjacks who brought
it down to the river and introduced it to the seafaring men.

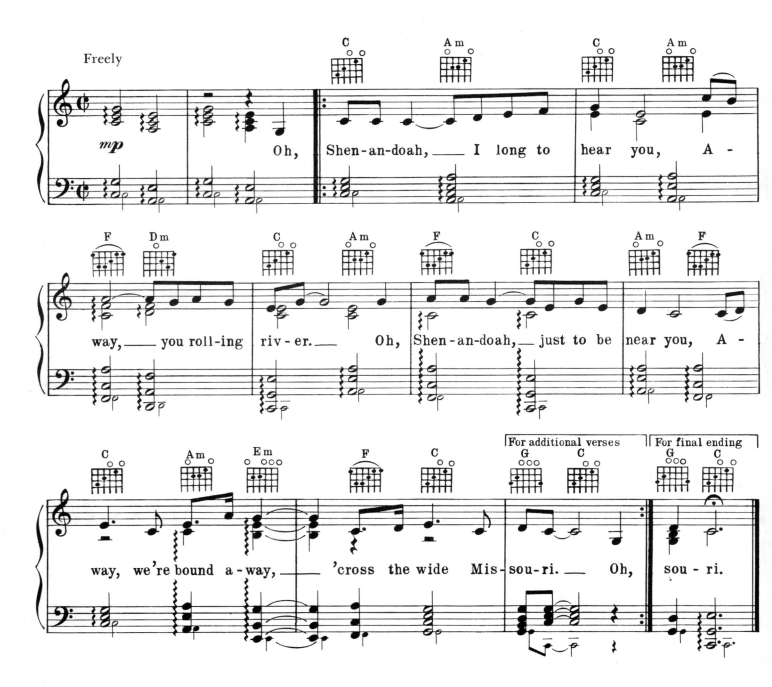

Oh, Shenandoah, I love your daughter,
Away, you rolling river.
Oh, Shenandoah, across the water,
Away, we're bound away,
'Cross the wide Missouri.

Oh, Shenandoah, I'm goin' to leave you,
Away, you rolling river.
Oh, Shenandoah, I won't deceive you,
Away, we're bound away,
'Cross the wide Missouri.

Careless Love

American Folk Song

Originally sung by southern mountain whites, this sorrowful tale was brought down to the Mississippi delta where it became identified with Negro dock workers. In 1921, W. C. Handy wrote his own version and called it "Loveless Love."

Slow blues

Love, oh love, oh Care-less Love, Love, oh love, oh Care-less Love, Love, _____

Love, oh love, oh Care-less Love, Just see what love has done to me.

Sorrow, sorrow, to my heart,
Sorrow, sorrow, to my heart,
Sorrow, sorrow, to my heart,
When me and my true love must part.

It's a pity that we met,
It's a pity that we met,
It's a pity that we met,
For those good times we'll never forget.

Now my money's spent and gone,
Now my money's spent and gone,
Now my money's spent and gone,
You passed my door a-singing a song.

Love my mama and my papa too,
Love my mama and my papa too,
Love my mama and my papa too,
But I'd leave them both and go with you.

Cried last night and the night before,
Cried last night and the night before,
Cried last night and the night before,
Going to cry tonight and I'll cry no more.

Oh, it's broke this heart of mine,
Oh, it's broke this heart of mine,
Oh, it's broke this heart of mine,
It'll break that heart of yours some time.

Red River Valley

Here's a switch: a Tin Pan Alley song that developed into a folk song. In 1896, songwriter James J. Kerrigan wrote a sentimental piece called "In the Bright Mohawk Valley." Pioneers heading westward picked up the tune, simplified the melody, and changed the lamenting lover to a cowboy and the locale to the Texas panhandle. With its loping four-four beat and open-air charm, "Red River Valley" sounds as authentic as any folk song that ever sprang from the sagebrush.

Traditional

Blue-Tail Fly

American Folk Song

Daniel Decatur Emmett may have been revered by the South as the composer of "Dixie," but his "Blue-Tail Fly" took such merry digs at indolent plantation owners that it was adopted as an Abolitionist song. Derived from Negro slave jingles, the ditty (originally called "Jimmy Crack Corn") was created in 1846 for a minstrel show.

And when he rode in the afternoon,
I follow with a hick'ry broom,
The pony being very shy
When bitten by the blue-tail fly.　(Refrain)

One day he rode around the farm,
The flies so numerous they did swarm;
One chanced to bite him on the thigh,
The devil take that blue-tail fly.　(Refrain)

The pony ran, he jumped, he pitched,
He threw my master in the ditch.
He died, the jury wondered why,
The verdict was the blue-tail fly.　(Refrain)

They laid him under a 'simmon tree,
His epitaph is there to see:
"Beneath this stone I'm forced to lie—
A victim of the blue-tail fly."　(Refrain)

Puff (The Magic Dragon)

Peter Yarrow, the Peter of Peter, Paul and Mary, shares one-half the credit for writing this gossamer fable and one-third for making it one of the durable delights of 1963. "Puff" remains a special favorite of children, while their elders take pleasure in finding hidden meanings in the frolicking of Puff and Jackie Paper.

Words and Music by Peter Yarrow and Leonard Lipton

Together they would travel on a boat with billowed sail.
Jackie kept a lookout perched on Puff's gigantic tail,
Noble kings and princes would bow whene'er they came,
Pirate ships would low'r their flag
      when Puff roared out his name. Oh! (Chorus)

A dragon lives forever but not so little boys,
Painted wings and giant rings make way for other toys.
One gray night it happened, Jackie Paper came no more
And Puff that mighty dragon,
    he ceased his fearless roar. Oh! (Chorus)

His head was bent in sorrow, green scales fell like rain.
Puff no longer went to play along the cherry lane.
Without his lifelong friend, Puff could not be brave
So Puff that mighty dragon,
    sadly slipped into his cave. Oh! (Chorus)

AURA LEE

The plaintive strains of "Aura Lee," a Civil War favorite, have also been heard under two other familiar titles. In 1865, with a new set of words, it became a West Point class song under the title of "Army Blues"; then, almost a hundred years after it was written, it re-emerged as the best-selling title song of Elvis Presley's movie Love Me Tender.

Words by W. W. Fosdick　　　　　　　　　　　　　**Music by G. R. Poulton**

Moderately, with expression

As the black-bird in the spring, be-neath the wil-low tree,

Sat and pip'd I heard him sing, _____ sing-ing "Au - ra Lee."

Au - ra Lee, Au - ra Lee, maid of gold-en hair!

Sun-shine came a - long with thee, and swal-lows in the air.

On Top of Old Smokey

American Folk Song

Though its roots were in England, "On Top of Old Smokey" first became known in America early in the 19th century when wagoneers sang it while driving their Conestoga wagons over treacherous pack trails. In 1963, Tom Glazer penned a variation, "On Top of Spaghetti," which, incredibly, became a hit.

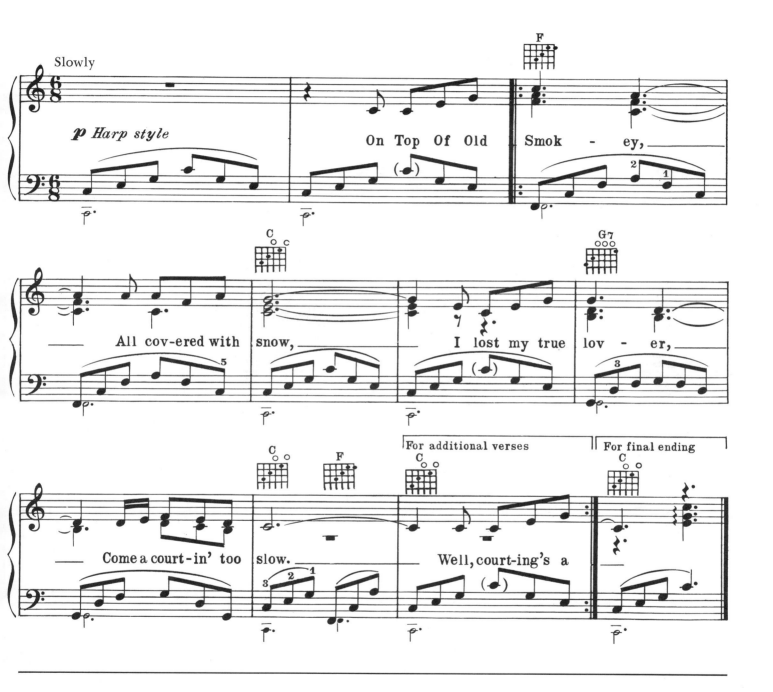

Well, courting's a pleasure,
But parting is grief,
And a false-hearted lover
Is worse than a thief.

A thief he will rob you
And take all you save,
But a false-hearted lover,
Will send you to your grave.

He'll hug you and kiss you
And tell you more lies
Than crossties on a railroad
Or the stars in the skies.

229

The Battle Hymn of the Republic

Words by
Julia Ward Howe

Music by
William Steffe

Majestic march tempo

Mine eyes have seen the glo-ry of the com-ing of the Lord; He is
tramp-ling out the vin-tage where the grapes of wrath are stored; He hath
loos'd the fate-ful light-ning of His ter-ri-ble swift sword, His truth is march-ing

On May 12, 1861, soon after the Civil War had begun, the strains of "John Brown's Body" were heard for the first time at Ft. Warren, near Boston. Adapted by C. S. Hall from a three-year-old Methodist hymn, "Say, Brothers, Will You Meet Us," the words to the new version referred not to the Harper's Ferry raider but to a Sgt. John Brown, then stationed at the fort. The song became so popular among Northern soldiers that opposition developed to so common a lyric being affixed to so exalted a melody. In 1862, Julia Ward Howe was persuaded to write the inspirational words we know as "The Battle Hymn of the Republic."

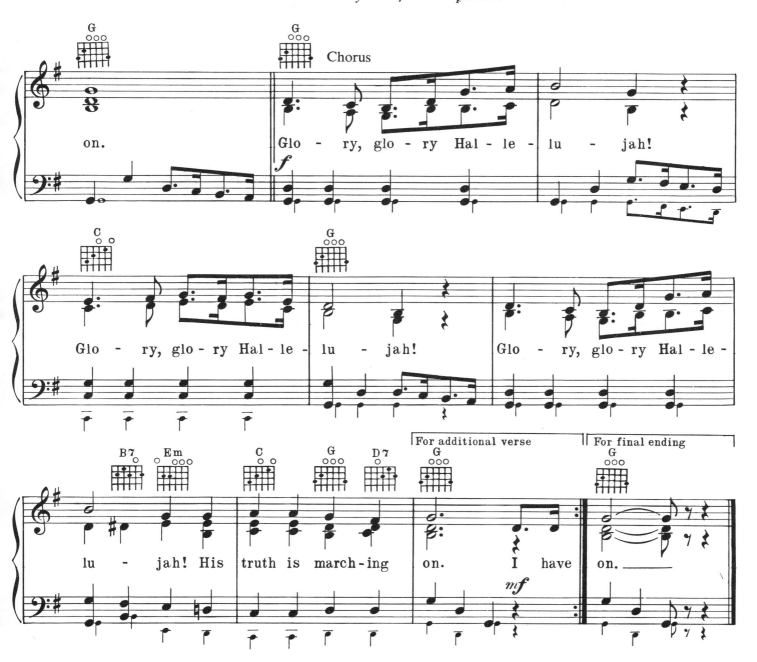

I have seen Him in the watch-fires of a hundred circling camps;
They have builded Him an altar in the evening dews and damps;
I can read His righteous sentence by the dim and flaring lamps,
His day is marching on.   (repeat Chorus)

I'll Walk with God

Though the familiar musical highlights of Sigmund Romberg's score for The Student Prince *were retained for the 1952 film version, Messrs. Webster and Brodszky were summoned to supply a suitable hymn for the grief-stricken prince as he views the bier of his dead father. "I'll Walk with God" was sung in the movie by the unseen Mario Lanza whose voice was dubbed in for actor Edmund Purdom.*

Words by Paul Francis Webster   Music by Nicholas Brodszky

Moderately, with deep emotion

I'll Walk With God ____ from this day on, His help-ing hand ____ I'll lean up-on; This is my prayer, ____ my hum-ble plea, ____ May the Lord be ev-er with me. ____ There is no

Rock of Ages

Words by Augustus M. Toplady
Music by Thomas Hastings

Augustus Toplady, a British clergyman, wrote a poem in 1776 called "A Living and Dying Prayer for the Holiest Believer in the World," and the prolific American composer Thomas Hastings set it to music in 1832. Along with "Nearer My God to Thee," this hymn, "Rock of Ages," is probably the most frequently performed piece at funerals.

Rock Of A-ges cleft for me, Let me hide my-self in thee; Let the water and the blood, From thy wound-ed side which flowed, Be of sin the dou-ble cure, Save from wrath and make me pure.

Could my tears forever flow, Could my zeal no languor know,
These for sin could not atone, Thou must save and Thou alone,
In my hand no price I bring, Simply to Thy cross I cling.

Faith of Our Fathers

In 1849, soon after Frederick Faber had left the Church of England in favor of the Church of Rome, he expressed his devotion to Catholicism in "Faith of Our Fathers." The text of the hymn has, however, since been revised. Now the term "faith," rather than referring to a particular religion, is made to apply to the teaching of Christ: "Love your enemies and pray for them that persecute you."

Words and Music by Frederick W. Faber, Henry F. Hemy and J. G. Walton

Faith Of Our Fa - thers! liv - ing still

In spite of dun - geon, fire____ and sword: O how our

hearts___ beat high___ with joy, When-e'er we hear that

glo - rious word: Faith Of Our Fa - thers, ho - ly

faith! We will be true to Thee till death.

A Mighty Fortress Is Our God

Martin Luther not only reformed the church, he also reformed the musical services, primarily by substituting German for the Latin text and arranging a new order for the Mass. An accomplished musician, he adapted many hymns, the most famous being his paraphrase of the 46th Psalm, "A Mighty Fortress." It was first published in 1529 and immediately became "The Battle Hymn of the Reformation," lifting the spirit and renewing the dedication of his followers.

Words by Martin Luther

Whispering Hope

"Alice Hawthorne" was really Septimus Winner, one of the most versatile writers of the mid-19th century. Winner went from the bird calls of "Listen to the Mocking Bird" to the doggerel nonsense of "Oh, Where, Oh, Where Has My Little Dog Gone?" to the gentle and optimistic "Whispering Hope."

Words and Music by Alice Hawthorne

Moderate waltz

Soft as the voice of an an - gel Breath-ing a les-son un-heard; _____ Hope with a gen-tle per - sua - sion Whis - pers her com-fort - ing word. _____ Wait till the dark-ness is o - ver, Wait till the tem-pest is

It is always a bit surprising to discover that Sir Arthur Sullivan—of Gilbert and Sullivan—was the composer of "Onward, Christian Soldiers." Originally, however, Rev. Baring-Gould had set his text to the accompaniment of the slow movement of the Haydn D-Major

ONWARD, CHRISTIAN SOLDIERS

Symphony and as such it was first sung at a Children's Festival in 1864. Haydn was discarded in favor of Sullivan as soon as his stirring melody was published seven years later. Today, it remains one of the most celebrated marching hymns ever written.

Words by Sabine Baring-Gould

Music by Sir Arthur Sullivan

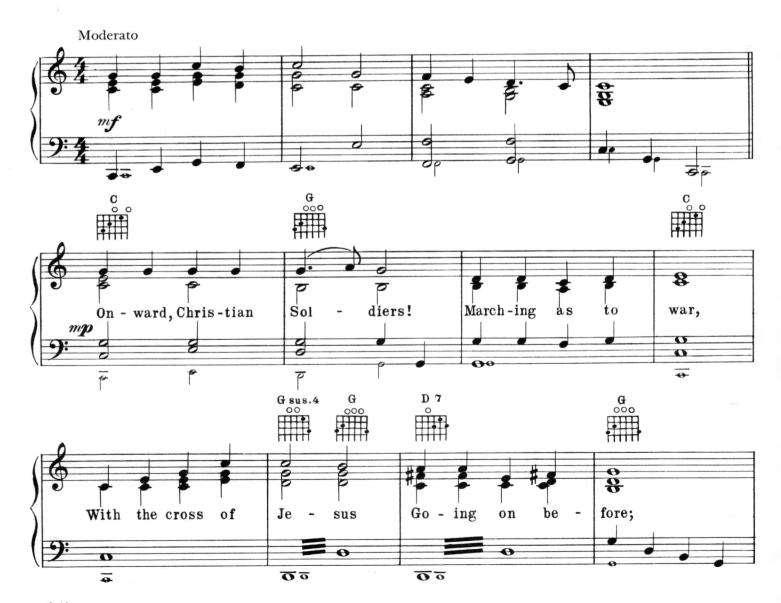

On-ward, Chris-tian Sol - diers! March-ing as to war,

With the cross of Je - sus Go-ing on be - fore;

Like a mighty army, Moves the Church of God:
Brothers, we are treading, Where the saints have trod;
We are not divided, All one body we,
One in hope, in doctrine, One in charity. (Chorus)

Onward then, ye people! Join our happy throng,
Blend with ours your voices In the triumph song;
Glory, laud and honor Unto Christ, the King,
This through countless ages Men and angels sing. (Chorus)

Abide with Me

In 1820, a young English clergyman, Henry Lyte, was visiting a dying friend who kept repeating the phrase "Abide with me." Moved by the visit, Lyte wrote the hymn but thought little about it until some 27 years later when, failing in health, he had the song published. It was not, however, until 1861 when organist William Monk added his own music to the words that the beauty of the work first became appreciated.

Words by Henry Lyte   **Music by W. H. Monk**

Swift to its close ebbs out life's little day,
Earth's joys grow dim, its glories pass away;
Change and decay in all around I see,
O Thou who changest not, abide with me.

America the Beautiful

Words by Katherine Lee Bates   **Music by Samuel A. Ward**

A trip to Pikes Peak, in 1893, inspired poetess Katherine Lee Bates to write these patriotic words. Later she set them to Samuel Ward's song, "O Mother Dear, Jerusalem."

O beautiful for pilgrim feet / Whose stern impassioned stress.
A thoroughfare for freedom beat / Across the wilderness.
America! America! God mend thine ev'ry flaw,
Confirm thy soul in self-control, / Thy liberty in law.

O beautiful for patriot dream / That sees beyond the years.
Thine alabaster cities gleam / Undimmed by human tears.
America! America! God shed his grace on thee,
And crown thy good with brotherhood / From sea to shining sea.

The Marines' Hymn

French composer Jacques Offenbach would certainly have been surprised. For it was his pulse-pounding march, "Couplets des deux Hommes d'Armes," sung in the 1868 opéra bouffe, Geneviève de Brabant, *that eventually served as the melody for "The Marines' Hymn." Which Leatherneck lyricist had the bright idea to match it to a tribute to the glories of the Marine Corps still remains a mystery, even though it was first published as recently as 1918. The line about the Halls of Montezuma refers to the Mexican War of 1847, while the shores of Tripoli recall the Marine activity against the Barbary pirates in 1805.*

Music by Jacques Offenbach

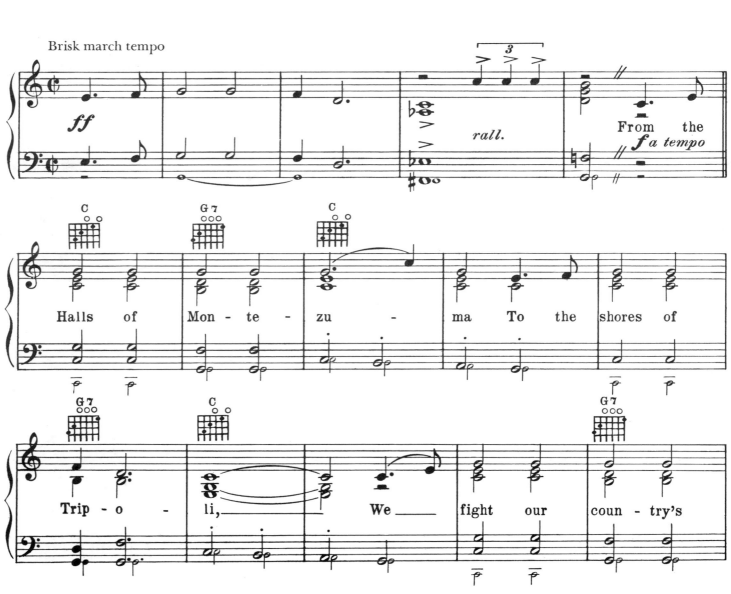

When Johnny Comes Marching Home

The thrill of welcoming home a soldier has never been more rousingly expressed than in this march, "When Johnny Comes Marching Home." Louis Lambert was the pseudonym of bandmaster Patrick Gilmore.

Words and Music by Louis Lambert

Get ready for the jubilee, Hurrah! Hurrah!
We'll give the heroes three times three, Hurrah! Hurrah!
The laurel wreath is ready now / To place upon his loyal brow,
And we'll all feel gay / When Johnny comes marching home!

America

The words of "America" were written in 1831 by Samuel Smith, a Boston clergyman, for a Fourth of July children's celebration.

Words by Samuel Francis Smith

Moderato

Our fathers' God, to Thee, / Author of liberty, / To thee we sing.
Long may our land be bright / With freedom's holy light;
Protect us by Thy might, / Great God, our King!

The Star Spangled Banner

On the morning of September 13, 1814, during the War of 1812, Francis Scott Key boarded a British warship in Chesapeake Bay under a flag of truce. His mission was to secure the release of a civilian held prisoner, but once aboard he was unable to leave because the fleet had begun its attack on Ft. McHenry. The bombardment lasted 25 hours. When the smoke had cleared the following morning, Key looked at the fort to discover that it had not surrendered, that "our flag was still there." He began scribbling a poem and completed it by the time he got to shore. Initially printed as "The Defence of Ft. McHenry" ("Tune—'Anacreon in Heaven'"), the title was later changed to "The Star Spangled Banner." On March 3, 1931, it became our official national anthem.

Words by Francis Scott Key

ram - parts we watched, were so gal - lant - ly stream - ing? And the rock - ets' red glare, the bombs burst - ing in air, Gave proof thro' the night that our flag was still there. Oh,— say, does that— Star Span - gled Ban - ner— yet— wave,— O'er the land— of the free and the home of the brave?

Chorus

9